To the Last Extremity

The Battles for Charleston, 1776–1782

by Mark Maloy

Dan Welch, series editor
Robert Orrison, chief historian

The Emerging Revolutionary War Series

offers compelling, easy-to-read overviews of some of the Revolutionary War's most important battles and stories.

Also part of the Emerging Revolutionary War Series:

A Single Blow: The Battles of Lexington and Concord and the Beginning of the American Revolution, April 19, 1775 by Phillip S. Greenwalt and Robert Orrison

A Handsome Flogging: The Battle of Monmouth, June 28, 1778 by William R. Griffith IV

The Winter that Won the War: The Winter Encampment at Valley Forge, 1777–1778 by Phillip S. Greenwalt

Unhappy Catastrophes: The American Revolution in Central New Jersey, 1776–1782 by Robert M. Dunkerly

Also by Mark Maloy

Victory or Death: The Battles of Trenton and Princeton, December 25, 1776–January 3, 1777

For a complete list of titles in the Emerging Revolutionary War Series, visit www.emergingrevolutionarywar.org

To the Last Extremity

The Battles for Charleston, 1776–1782

by Mark Maloy

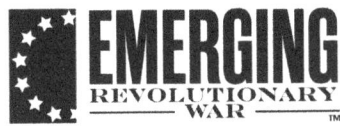

Savas Beatie
California

First edition, first printing

ISBN-13: 978-1-61121-643-1 (paperback)
ISBN-13: 978-1-61121-644-8 (ebook)

Names: Maloy, Mark, author. Title: To the last extremity : the battles for Charleston, 1776-1782 / by Mark Maloy.
Other titles: Battles for Charleston, 1776-1782
Description: El Dorado Hills, CA : Savas Beatie, [2023] | Series: Emerging Revolutionary War series | Includes bibliographical references. | Summary: "In this book, historian Mark Maloy not only recounts the Revolutionary War history of Charleston, he takes you to the places where the history actually happened. He shows you where the outnumbered Patriots beat back the most powerful navy in the world, where soldiers bravely defended the city in 1779 and 1780, and where thousands suffered under occupation"-- Provided by publisher.
Identifiers: LCCN 2022043897 | ISBN 9781611216431 (paperback) | ISBN 9781611216448 (ebook)
Subjects: LCSH: Charleston (S.C.)--History--Revolution, 1775-1783--Campaigns. | South Carolina--History--Revolution, 1775-1783--Battlefields--Tours. | Historic sites--South Carolina--Charleston Region--Tours. | Charleston (S.C.)--Tours
Classification: LCC E241.C4 M25 2022 | DDC 975.7/91503--dc23/ eng/20221104 LC record available at https://lccn.loc.gov/2022043897

SB

Published by
Savas Beatie LLC
989 Governor Drive, Suite 102
El Dorado Hills, California 95762
916-941-6896
sales@savasbeatie.com
www.savasbeatie.com

Savas Beatie titles are available at special discounts for bulk purchases in the United States by corporations, institutions, and other organizations. For more details, you may e-mail us at sales@savasbeatie.com, or visit our website at www.savasbeatie.com for additional information.

To my sons: Samuel Washington Maloy and Thomas Mercer Maloy.

I hope one day, you too will find inspiration from the heroes of the past . . .

Table of Contents

List of Maps

Maps by Edward Alexander

Footnotes for the volume are available at
https://emergingrevolutionarywar.org/emerging-revolutionary-war-series/to-the-last-extremity-footnotes/

Acknowledgments

    I would like to acknowledge the many people who have helped make this publication possible.

    To historians Phillip Greenwalt and Robert Orrison at Emerging Revolutionary War. Phill and Rob have been extremely supportive and gave great insights throughout the creation of this book. Thanks to them for creating Emerging Revolutionary War, which has become a great outlet for myself and others to write about the American Revolution and connect the stories to the places where they occurred. What started as just a blog has grown to include a book series, social media platform, live shows, podcasts, documentary appearances, and bus tours. More important than my professional connection with them, their friendship I have found to be the most rewarding part. Thanks also to Emerging Revolutionary War authors and contributors Billy Griffith, Kevin Pawlak, and Dan Welch who were always a great sounding board for ideas.

    Thanks to Mark Wilcox, who along with Rob and Phill, joined me on a research trip to the Low Country to explore the sites associated with the battles of Charleston. Being able to show a first-time visitor a place I enjoy so much always reinvigorates my love of a place and desire to share places with more people. And to Dave and Blair Dellenbach who gave me a home base in Charleston while working on the book but, more importantly, have been good friends of my wife and me since 2008.

To Theodore Savas and the Savas Beatie team who have given me the opportunity to tell this incredible story. Thank you for your help throughout the process of authoring my second book. I'm proud to be an author in their ranks and love seeing the numerous other books published by a great press that highlights the importance of military history in our national story.

To Gordy Morgan for editing the manuscript. Gordy greatly improved the wording of sentences and made my thoughts much more concise and impactful. The book is much better thanks to his careful eye.

To my copy editor, Leon Reed, for an excellent job of editing and helping get the final text across the finish line. Leon also helped to make the final text much more succinct and clearer.

A Moultrie flag proudly flies in downtown Charleston. (mm)

To Veronica Kane for laying out this volume. She did a fantastic job of making this book come to life.

To my friend, Dan Welch, who provided excellent edits and helped shuttle the book across the finish line.

To Edward Alexander, who did an incredible job of creating the maps for the book. I love maps in military history books, and Ed did incredible work and I hope gives the reader a much better appreciation of what happened and where it happened.

To Rick Wise for reviewing the manuscript. Rick provided great input and helped to clarify many points in the book. He is doing great work in helping preserve Revolutionary War history in South Carolina.

To Carl Borick, Director of the Charleston Museum, for all his work on Charleston's Revolutionary War history and reviewing the manuscript. Carl first piqued my interest in the 1780 Revolutionary War history of Charleston at a talk he gave back in 2008. His books on the Revolution are essential reading, and his work in telling the city's history at the Charleston Museum is exemplary.

To the entire Charleston history community. Having worked for public history sites in the Charleston area, it has a great network of public historians. Especially meaningful in my learning to understand South Carolina history were my coworkers

A view of downtown Charleston from the steeple of St. Michael's Church. The church was built in the 1750s and witnessed the Revolutionary War. George Washington looked out on this view from the steeple when he visited in 1791. (mm)

at Middleton Place plantation, including Ron Vido, Daniel Gidick, Bob Sherman, Jeff Chilcote, and Joel Anderson.

To my fellow reenactors in the 7th Virginia Regiment of the Continental Line. Reenacting battles in the same place where the history happened is one of the best ways to connect with the history and get a small taste of what their lives were like. Reenacting the siege of Charleston in 2005 and living histories at Fort Moultrie were particularly educational and enjoyable.

To my fellow Park Rangers in the National Park Service who have helped me grow as a historian. Working at many of America's most important historic sites is a great honor and the conversations and debates about historical topics with my coworkers throughout my career have truly encouraged my devotion to interpreting our nation's history to the public. Specifically, from my time at Fort Sumter and Fort Moultrie National Historic Site: Dawn Davis, Gary Alexander, Jennifer Zoebelein, Jeff Black, Jeff Jones, and Nate Johnson, who helped instill in me a love for the history of Charleston and the National Park Service.

To Rick Hatcher, whom I was honored to invite to write the foreword for the book. Having had the privilege of working with him as an intern at Fort Sumter and Fort Moultrie National Historic Site in 2009, it was a true honor to be able to have him introduce this story.

To my friends and family, who know all too well my love of Charleston and its history. Like a European city, Charleston is filled with layers of history, each more fascinating than the next. Special thanks to my siblings (Michael, Brigid, and Molly) who have been a great support system throughout the writing of this book. Thanks also to Cliff Conaty, a good family friend, who was very supportive throughout my time in Charleston, may he rest in peace.

To my parents, Mary and Pat. Their taking me to Charleston as a young adult to visit some of these sites for the first time, infused a love for the area that determined my move there after college. Thank you for supporting my love of history and encouraging me to follow my dreams.

To my wife, Lauren. This book would not be possible without her. She has routinely given me time and space to write this book and support my involvement with Emerging Revolutionary War, all while being pregnant with our second son, Thomas. She is an amazing wife and mother. Thank you for all you do!

To my sons, Samuel and Thomas. I hope they find inspiration in these stories and places. I have always found the history of Charleston in the Revolution, despite its many thorns, a beautiful story of perseverance and courage. It is my earnest wish they come to learn what I have discovered: that it is history that teaches us to hope.

Finally, to the men who sacrificed around Charleston during the war so that we might have the country we know and love today. Though often overlooked, I hope this book encourages more Americans to delve into the stories of these true American heroes. We are truly the beneficiaries of their loss and sacrifice. I always keep John Adams words in mind when he wrote in 1777:

"Posterity! You will never know how much it cost the present generation to preserve your freedom! I hope you will make a good use of it. If you do not, I shall repent in Heaven, that I ever took half the pains to preserve it."

PHOTO CREDITS: **College of Charleston (cc); Caroline County Historical Society (chs);** *Harper's Weekly* **(hw); Library of Congress (loc); Mark Maloy (mm); Mark Wilcox (mw); Metropolitan Museum of Art (mma); New York Public Library (nypl); Phillip S. Greenwalt (psg); Wikipedia (wiki)**

For the Emerging Revolutionary War Series

Theodore P. Savas, *publisher*
Dan Welch, *series editor*
Robert Orrison, *chief historian and co-founder*
Sarah Keeney, *editorial consultant*

Maps by Edward Alexander
Design and layout by Veronica Kane

Touring Revolutionary War Charleston

"The beauty of Charleston is guaranteed to captivate the visitor, but there is also something about the landscape that holds the memory."

— Historian John Keegan

Charleston, South Carolina, is one of the most beautiful cities in the country. Known for its sandy beaches and highly rated Southern cuisine, it is a major tourist destination in the United States. Located on the east coast at the confluence of the Ashley and Cooper Rivers, the city was founded by English settlers in 1670. One of the major southern port cities, it saw significant action in both the Revolutionary War and the American Civil War. Having survived two wars, multiple fires, a catastrophic earthquake in 1886, and countless storms and hurricanes, the city is remarkably well preserved. Walking through historic Charleston, the sight of hundreds of 18th- and 19th-century buildings will transport you back in time. The sound of horse hooves clopping on the city streets echoes off the buildings and sea breezes shake the fronds of the numerous palmetto trees. Tourists stop to read signs and placards that note the numerous historic sites, and they enjoy historic tours of the city. Although remembered for its history as the "Cradle of the Confederacy" and the site of the first shots of the American Civil War, the city's Revolutionary War history is less well known.

One of the largest and wealthiest cities in British colonial America, Charleston in 1776 played a critical role in the American War for Independence and an essential role in the creation of the United States. In fact, the state of South Carolina proved indispensable in the bloody eight-year conflict. Charleston and its environs were the home to numerous Patriots (as well as Loyalists) and was the scene of a major battle, a protracted siege, and numerous skirmishes.

The state of South Carolina vies with New Jersey and New York for the distinction of having the most battles fought within their borders during the Revolutionary War. One author has said, "South Carolina is to the Revolution what Virginia is to the War for Southern Independence." This may be surprising to people today who often know only the extensive Civil War history of South Carolina, but reminders of the Revolution can be found throughout the charming city of Charleston today.

This book is an attempt to relate some of the most notable moments of the Revolutionary War in Charleston and show where you can go to see and learn about that history today. The book focuses largely on the battle of Sullivan's Island and the Siege of Charleston, but I will also examine the many other skirmishes that occurred in the immediate area. This is by no means meant to serve as any kind of definitive book on the Revolution in Charleston, but it is hoped the reader will gain a good overview of the events and consult the "Suggested Reading" section to find where they can learn more information about the battles described here. It is hoped that readers will be inspired by this book to want to read more and also to visit the sites where these events occurred, as there is no substitute to standing in the footsteps of the people of the past.

On Sullivan's Island, while the sands and water have changed over time and the original palmetto fort is long gone, the National Park Service interprets the history of the battle on the original site. In downtown Charleston, there are very few tangible reminders of the siege of

The Charleston Battery as viewed from the harbor. (mm)

Charleston that occurred in 1780; the area where so much of the combat occurred is now a very popular and trendy part of downtown. In Marion Square, only one small piece of the Hornwork remains from the massive number of trenches and ditches built there in 1780. Where the blood of many American Patriots and British soldiers was spilled is now filled with houses, restaurants, and bars—people spend their lives here not knowing the amazing story of what happened directly under their feet almost 250 years ago.

In May of 2010, I had the honor to spearhead the installation of a state historic marker denoting the location of the surrender of the American troops in May 1780. Hopefully, more historic markers, signs, and monuments will be added to the cultural landscape in the future. In recent years it has become, unfortunately, more and more acceptable to remove or destroy historic monuments to people who do not share the same values as 21st-century Americans, and in Charleston, this has included the removal of a monument to a United States Vice President, largely because of his views on race and slavery. No doubt, many of the American Patriots (and British and Loyalist soldiers for that matter) described in the following narrative held similarly abhorrent views on those issues, but we should try to understand the figures of the past within the context of their time and elevate and honor the positive contributions they provided us as the beneficiaries of their work and sacrifice.

I hope this book will encourage people to visit Charleston and appreciate the city's rich history. For those who live there, I hope they continue to advocate for more preservation and interpretation of its truly glorious past. A missing piece in the commemorative landscape is a fitting monument or memorial to the more than 800 Continental soldiers who perished as prisoners of war in Charleston harbor for the cause of American liberty.

Luckily, the South Carolina Liberty Trail, a joint effort between the South Carolina Battleground Preservation Trust and the American Battlefield Trust, is working to preserve and interpret dozens of Revolutionary War sites across the Palmetto state (including Charleston) as we approach the 250th anniversary of the conflict. The more preservation and interpretation of these sites, the longer the stories of the past will live on.

Charleston is a beautiful city, and the climate is perfect to visit at any time. I would suggest, though, that spring and summer—during the anniversaries of the major engagements and battles—mark the best time to visit.

In this volume you will find three different tours of the Revolutionary War battles around Charleston. They will take you to some of the most significant Revolutionary War sites in the Charleston area. The first tour mostly covers the northern side of the harbor, focusing largely on the battle of Sullivan's Island. This

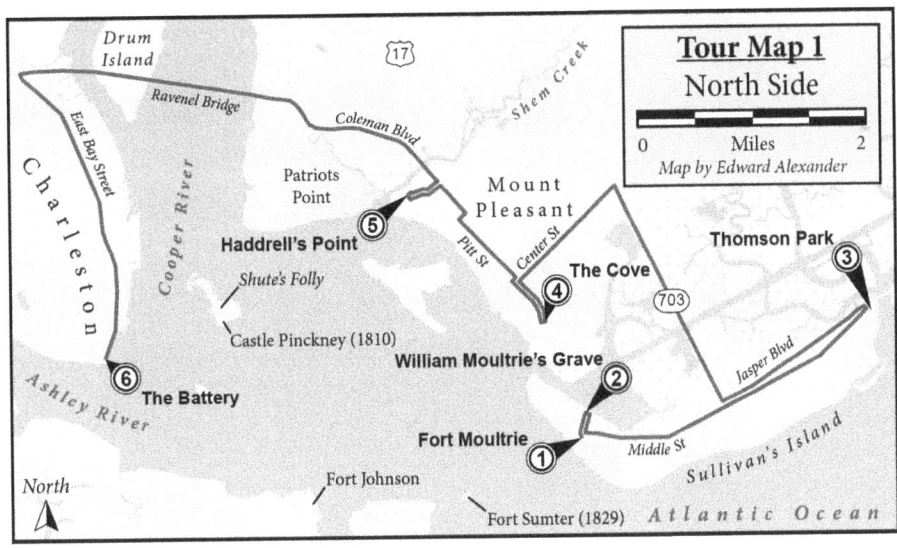

NORTH SIDE DRIVING TOUR—This map depicts the modern area where you can drive and see sites related to the June 28, 1776, battle for Sullivan's Island. The numbers correspond with stops you can read about in Chapter Two.

is a driving tour that takes you to the major sites of 1776, beginning at Fort Moultrie, then traversing Sullivan's Island and Mount Pleasant and ending in downtown Charleston.

The second tour is a driving tour of the south side of the harbor. It begins at Stono Ferry and then goes across James Island, West Ashley, Summerville, and North Charleston. Here you will see sites associated with the 1779 attack on Charleston and the British advance on the city in 1780, among others.

The third tour is a walking tour of downtown Charleston. It begins at the outermost British siege lines from 1780 and continues all the way through downtown to the Battery. This is a very long walk, so feel free to break it up as you see fit. Like the Freedom Trail in Boston, this route is lined not only with great historic sites, but numerous bars and restaurants. The best way to experience downtown Charleston is to wander the streets and closely explore the buildings and the history.

A brief note on terminology in this book. I use the modern name of the city throughout this book. Before 1783, the city was called Charles Town or Charlestowne. In 1783, it was officially renamed Charleston. For the sake of simplicity and to avert confusion, I have decided to use the modern version of Charleston throughout, unless in quotes from

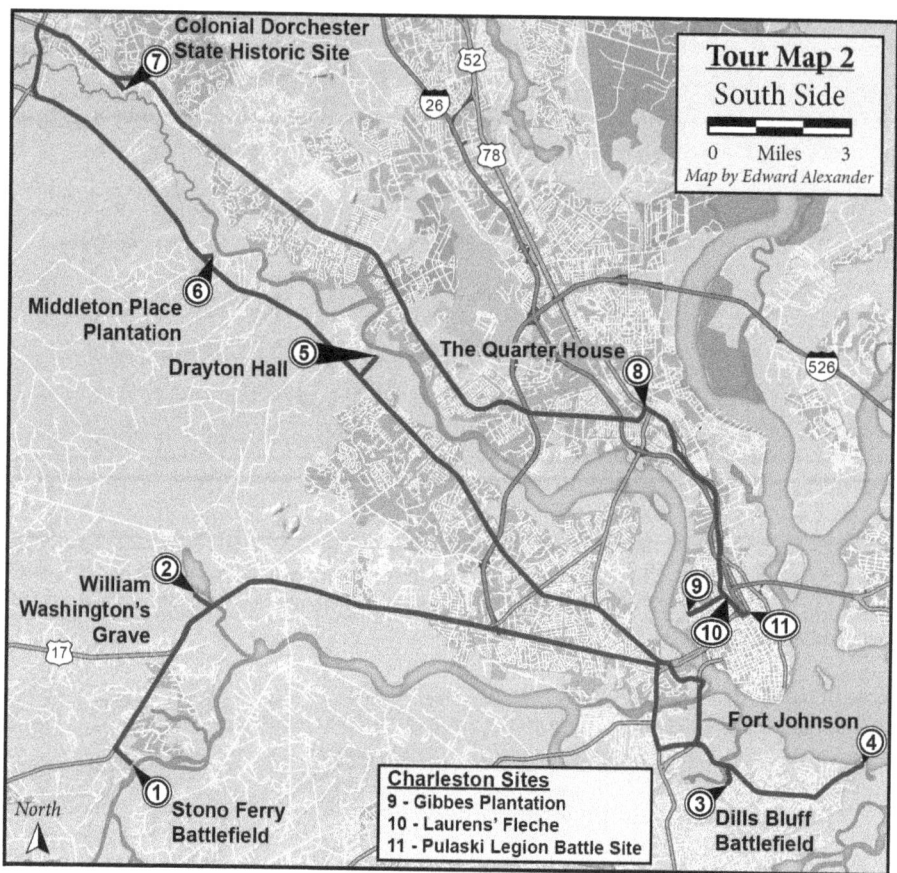

SOUTH SIDE DRIVING TOUR—This map depicts the modern area where you can drive and see sites related to Prevost's invasion in 1779 and the advance of Clinton's army in 1780. The numbers correspond with stops in Chapters Four and Five.

primary sources. Throughout the book I use the term Americans and Patriots to describe those who were fighting for the cause of American independence. Although most Americans at the time identified more with their states and the armies were often made up of diverse arrays of people from different countries. Many Americans also sided with the Crown forces, and I describe these men as Loyalists, even though and many of them simply saw themselves as patriots. For the Crown forces, I use the term British, even though large portions of their army were made up of Irish, American, and German soldiers. I use these terms for simplicity and style reasons. However, as any historian knows, the history is always much more complicated than often seen on the surface.

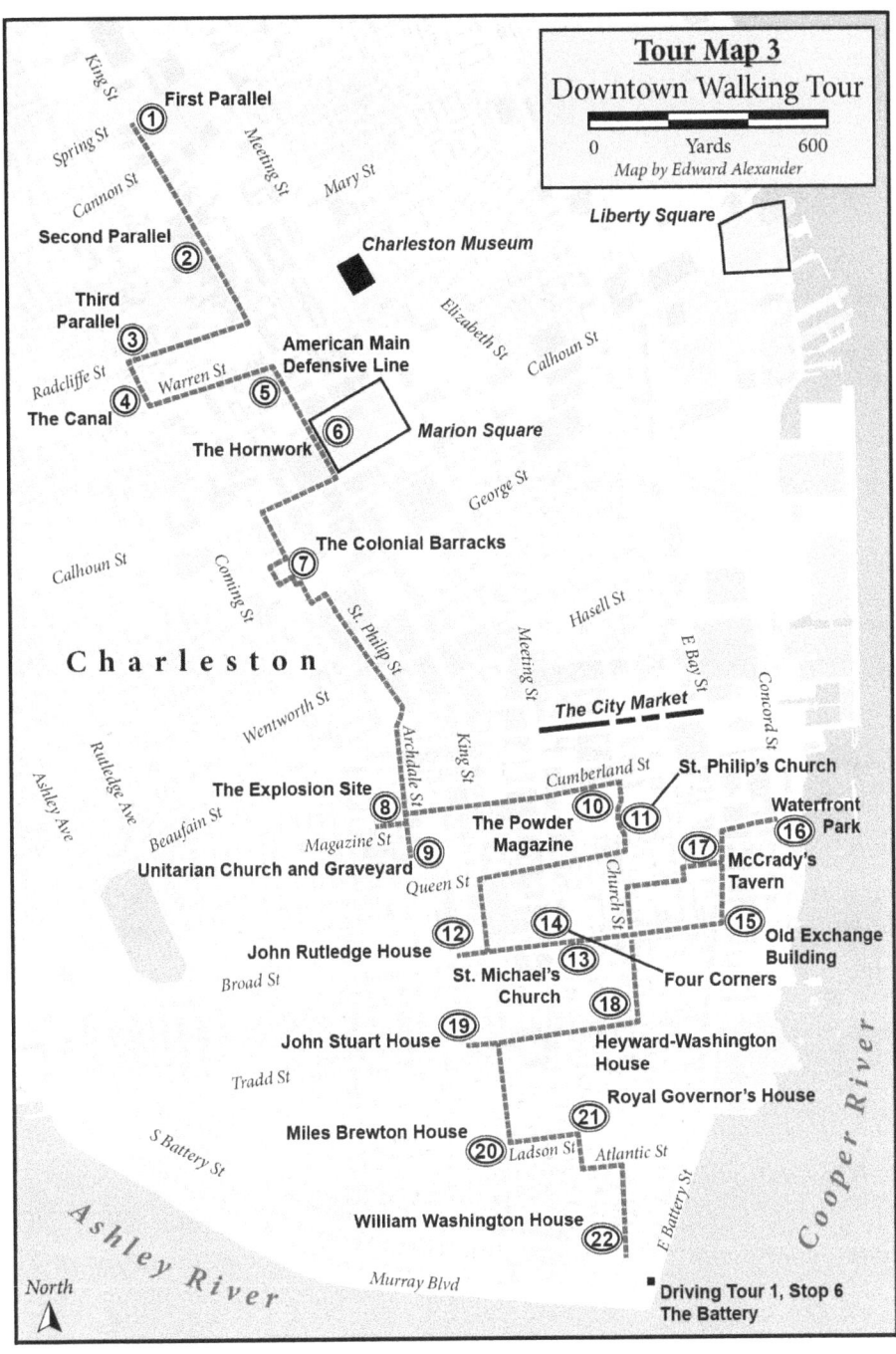

DOWNTOWN WALKING TOUR—This map depicts downtown Charleston and the main sites related to the Revolutionary War. The numbers correspond with stops in Chapters Six through Eight.

$\mathcal{F}oreword$

BY RICHARD HATCHER III

April 19, 2025, will mark the 250th anniversary of the battles of Lexington and Concord in Massachusetts. At Concord, "The shot heard round the world" ignited the American War for Independence. In the eight years following those commemorations, national attention will be focused on the best-known events that occurred between 1775 and 1783. Among them certainly will be the battle of Bunker Hill, the Declaration of Independence, the 1777–78 winter at Valley Forge, and the siege of Yorktown. And finally, on September 3, 2033, we will commemorate the 250th anniversary of the Treaty of Paris, which ended the war and forced Great Britain to recognize the sovereignty of the United States of America.

Many more significant events and military actions will be recognized by states and localities during the eight-year commemoration. Battles occurred in every one of the original thirteen colonies, with additional military actions taking place in the modern-day states of Tennessee, Arkansas, Indiana, Illinois, Kentucky, Alabama, Ohio, and Florida. More than 200 separate skirmishes and battles each were fought within New York, New Jersey, and South Carolina. Two of the most significant occurred in South Carolina—the June 28, 1776, battle of Sullivan's Island and the April 1–May 12, 1780, siege of Charleston.

The battle of Sullivan's Island stands as one of the first major American victories in the war. A small force of South Carolina infantry and artillery defeated both the British Army and Royal Navy in their attempt to capture Charleston. Word of the victory reached

Looking down Broad Street toward St. Michael's Church in downtown Charleston. St. Michaels, dating to 1761, was a witness to the events of the Revolutionary War in Charleston. (mm)

A view of Charleston Harbor immediately following the battle on June 28, 1776. (nypl)

Philadelphia on July 20, 1776, less than two weeks after the Second Continental Congress had approved the final draft of the Declaration of Independence and its printing. News of the victory could not have come at a better time, raising the morale of the members of the Second Continental Congress. John Hancock, alone, signed the Declaration on July 4 and the rest of the Congress began signing it on August 2.

Four years later, Charleston was again the focus of a British siege. In 1780, British forces besieged Charleston and captured the city on May 12, 1780. John Adams described it as "The severest blow we ever received," the worst Patriot defeat of the war. The surrender resulted in the loss of the new nation's fourth-largest city, and the capture of the southern American army. More than 5,600 officers and men (including 3,400 or so Continental Line veterans from Virginia, North Carolina, and South Carolina) were captured and imprisoned, and 400 cannon were lost. This loss stands only behind the surrender of the U.S. Army's garrison of 12,500 at Harpers Ferry, September 15, 1862, and the surrender of 12,000 U.S. soldiers in the Philippines on April 9, 1942.

A view of Charleston as it appeared in 1762. (nypl)

Mark Maloy's publication, *To the Last Extremity: The Battles for Charleston, 1776–1782*, has presented readers

Charleston, South Carolina in 1774. (nypl)

with not only a clear and well-written history of the events leading up to and the battle of Sullivan's Island, but also of the years between the victory and the 1780 siege and capture of Charleston. Maloy paints a vivid picture of postwar Charleston, including the 1791 visit of President George Washington. To complete his work, the author provides a driving tour of the city's pertinent Revolutionary War sites and locations for those who find themselves visiting the Holy City.

RICHARD HATCHER III is the former historian for Fort Sumter and Fort Moultrie National Historical Park.

"... animated only with the sacred love of liberty ..."
— John Hancock about the defenders of Charleston, 1776

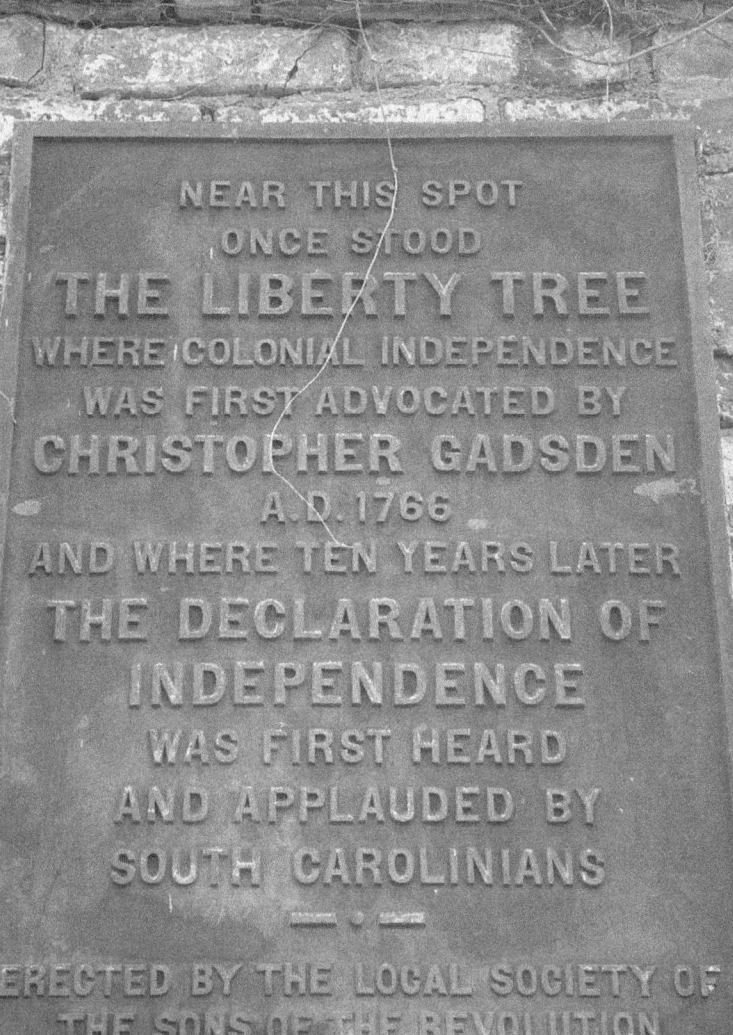

NEAR THIS SPOT
ONCE STOOD
THE LIBERTY TREE
WHERE COLONIAL INDEPENDENCE
WAS FIRST ADVOCATED BY
CHRISTOPHER GADSDEN
A.D. 1766
AND WHERE TEN YEARS LATER
THE DECLARATION OF
INDEPENDENCE
WAS FIRST HEARD
AND APPLAUDED BY
SOUTH CAROLINIANS
— · —
ERECTED BY THE LOCAL SOCIETY OF
THE SONS OF THE REVOLUTION
A.D. 1905

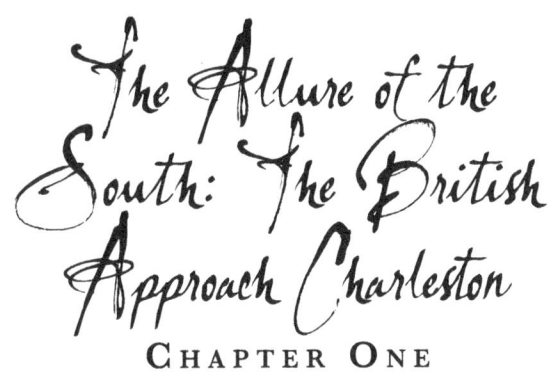

The Allure of the South: The British Approach Charleston

CHAPTER ONE

1776

"I dare think the battery at Sullivan's Island will not discharge two rounds"

— Patrick Tonyn, royal governor of
British Florida, 1776

Charleston (at that time called Charles Town or Charlestowne), South Carolina, seemed an unlikely place for rebellion against the British Crown. The colony of South Carolina had benefited greatly from being part of the British Empire and was one of the wealthiest colonies in North America. Much of that fortune was centered in the Lowcountry, the area around Charleston near the sea. Here the main cash crop of rice, cultivated by thousands of African-American slaves (who prior to the American Revolution outnumbered the white population in the colony) made southern planters extremely prosperous. The southern planter families were essentially American royalty.

However, as South Carolinians saw the way the King and Parliament treated their fellow colonists in Massachusetts after their protests on taxes, many South Carolina planters soon asserted their rights as Englishmen. Like colonists in Massachusetts, Charleston Patriots had a "liberty tree" that became a central place for protests against British authority, and, in 1773 and 1774, the Patriots of Charleston held a few "tea parties" of their own that resulted in either the destruction or securing of British tea to protest taxes that were levied by the Crown. However, when Patriots dumped British tea into Boston Harbor, the Crown cracked down hard on the colony of Massachusetts. In 1774, the British closed the entire port of Boston, essentially crippling their

The site of the old "liberty tree" in Charleston is marked at 80 Alexander Street downtown. After conquering the city in 1780, the British sought out this oak tree and chopped it down. (mm)

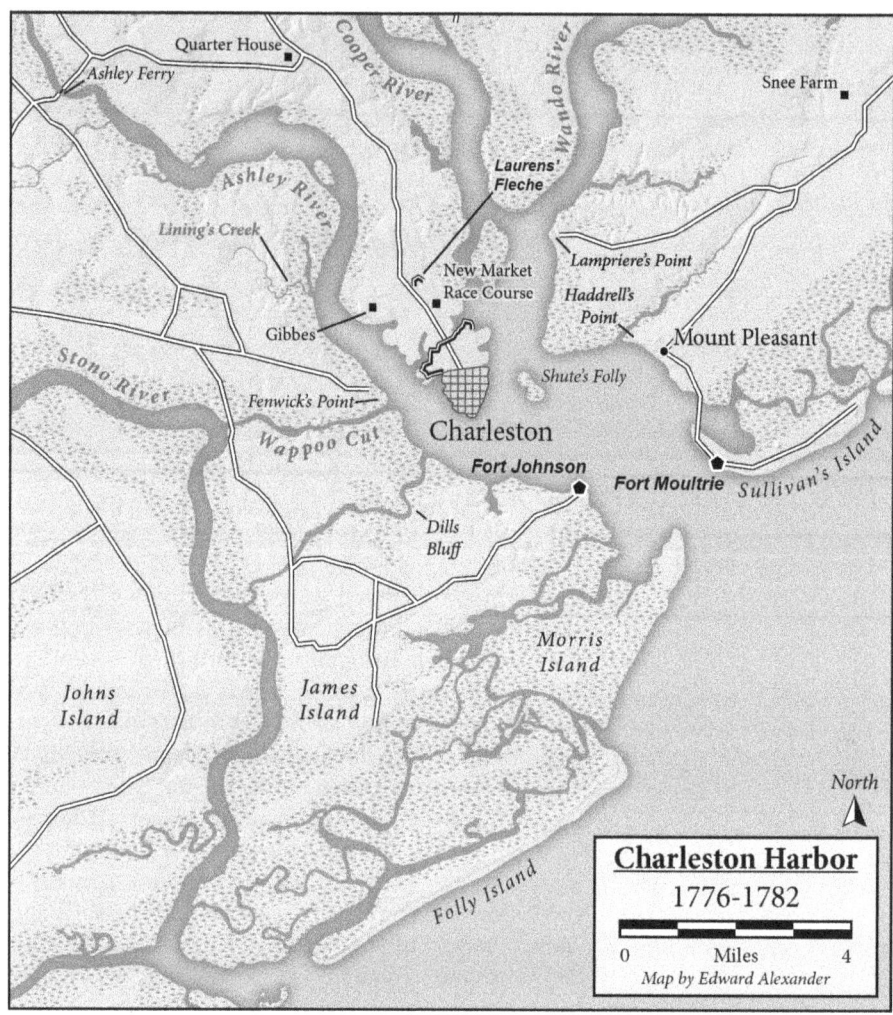

CHARLESTON HARBOR —This map gives a good view of the terrain immediately surrounding Charleston during the Revolutionary War. The rivers, islands, roads, and forts would play critical roles in how armies and navies maneuvered in the area during the war.

main industry. Many of the other colonies, including South Carolina, recoiled in horror at the prospect of the British Navy shutting down their ports. Realizing that the Crown was becoming a threat to their liberty, Patriot citizens quickly created a "provincial congress" that would act as a new de facto government for South Carolina apart from the Royal government in the colony. Not ready for full independence from Great Britain, the South Carolinians, along with many other Americans, hoped to reconcile their differences and secure their liberty while staying in the British Empire.

They sent delegates to a Continental Congress in Philadelphia with representatives from many of the American colonies in hopes of negotiating with the Crown while they began in earnest to prepare for the defense of their homes from the potential wrath of the British Empire.

In April 1775, the first shots of the Revolutionary War were fired at Lexington and Concord outside of Boston, Massachusetts. Shortly after this, the Continental Congress authorized the raising of a Continental army for the defense of the colonies in the summer of 1775. When George Washington of Virginia was named the commander in chief, he went to Boston to take command of the northern army that was laying siege to that city. As the idea of independence gained support in South Carolina in 1775, the royal governor and British authorities unsuccessfully tried to clamp down on Patriot resistance. That summer, the South Carolina provincial government in Charleston raised regiments of soldiers to defend the people of South Carolina. These regiments later became part of the Southern Department of the Continental army.

The royal governor of South Carolina, Lord William Campbell, did as much as he could to restore British rule. However, by September 15, 1775, he feared for his safety, and that night he fled his home at 34 Meeting Street and escaped to a British ship

The view of the Ashley River from the ruins of the Middleton Place Plantation house. Hundreds of rice plantations surrounded the city of Charleston at the time of the Revolutionary War. Today, some of these plantations, like Middleton Place, are open to the public. (mm)

The view of the large private homes along the Battery in Charleston. Most of these homes that line East Bay Street near the battery are from the 19th century, but display the wealth and prosperity the city enjoyed from the colonial period up until the mid-nineteenth century. (mm)

in Charleston Harbor. He would ultimately return to England, but not before participating in the British attempt to retake Charleston. In 1776, the colonial government of South Carolina created a new constitution and provincial government, and Charlestonian John Rutledge became its new president.

While many in the Lowcountry began to embrace the new American cause, many others decided to remain loyal to King George III. Many of the slaves in the colony looked for opportunities to escape and join the British. In Virginia, the royal governor, Lord Dunmore, proclaimed in November of 1775 that all slaves of rebel masters who joined the British side would receive their freedom.

Many of the lower-class whites who resented the landed gentry looked to use this coming conflict to settle old scores and advance themselves by fighting on the side of the British. And many American Indian tribes, on the frontiers of South Carolina, looked to side with the British with hopes of reclaiming their ancestral lands.

This divided state of South Carolina increased the potential for conflict and made the colony an appealing place for the British to launch an assault early in the war. Or so they thought. By the end of 1775, with a stalemate around the city of Boston, the British began to think of subduing other rebellious areas of North America, and now looked toward the southern colonies. With about 12,000 residents in 1776, Charleston was the largest city in the South and the fourth largest in America. It seemed to the British high command that if they could capture Charleston,

The last royal governor of South Carolina, Lord William Campbell, fled Charleston in September of 1775. (wiki)

This drawing of the skyline of Charleston was done in 1774. The skyline today is remarkably similar. Today you can still see the steeple of St. Michael's Church and the Old Exchange Building. (loc)

order would soon be restored in the empire, or at least in the South.

The city of Charleston sat at the end of a peninsula where the Ashley and Cooper Rivers met and emptied into Charleston Harbor and the Atlantic Ocean. To the south were James and Johns Islands, and to the east of the city was Mount Pleasant. At the entrance of Charleston Harbor was Morris Island on the southern side and Sullivan's Island on the northern side.

Fort Johnson was on the southern side of the harbor on James Island. Fort Johnson would later gain notoriety as the location from which the first shot of the American Civil War was fired in 1861, but in 1776 it was the primary fort guarding Charleston Harbor from naval attack. It was built of tabby (a type of concrete made with oyster shells and lime); South Carolina soldiers captured the fort in 1775 and raised the first flag of American liberty over it. This flag, designed by Col. William Moultrie, was blue with a white crescent in the top left corner. The blue was the same color as the coats his soldiers wore, and the crescent was an ancient heraldry symbol denoting second-born sons and an increasing prospect of a brighter future. With Patriot cannon now at Fort Johnson and at the southern tip of the peninsula in the city itself, an additional fort on the north side of the harbor would force any British vessels to run a gauntlet between the two forts if they tried to enter the harbor.

John Rutledge, president of South Carolina, learning that an expedition of British troops and ships would soon head towards Charleston, ordered the 1st and 2nd South Carolina Regiments to begin

While none of the original walls of Fort Johnson still exist, visitors to the site can still see a brick powder magazine from the Revolutionary War. This magazine was buried by Confederate soldiers during the American Civil War, which had the unintended consequence of preserving the structure. (mm)

constructing a new fort on Sullivan's Island, outside of the city, guarding the approach to the harbor.

In December 1775, the Patriots occupied the area known as Haddrell's Point in Mount Pleasant, and by January captured Sullivan's Island, which had become a refuge for escaped slaves and loyalists. Colonel William Moultrie, commanding the 2nd South Carolina Regiment, described Sullivan's Island in 1776 as "quite a wilderness, and a thick deep swamp . . . covered with live oak, myrtle, and palmetto trees."

Colonel Moultrie and the 2nd South Carolina would oversee constructing this new fort on Sullivan's

This plaque denotes the site of Fort Johnson as where Colonel William Moultrie first raised his liberty flag on September 15, 1775. (mm)

While William Moultrie's original flag no longer exists, he described it in his memoirs as a " . . . large blue flag made with a crescent in the dexter corner . . ." Some versions have the crescent upright, some tilted, and some with the word LIBERTY written across the bottom of the flag or within the crescent. This flag became the basis of the modern South Carolina flag. Today, a replica of the original flag flies over William Moultrie's grave. (mm)

Island. The plan he laid out was massive, and hundreds of slaves were contracted out from their masters to begin the arduous task of digging, cutting, and building the breastworks in the hot Carolina sun. It would be a square defensive position with diamonds on each corner. Each wall would measure 500 feet long and 16 feet thick. The fort would be constructed using two stacks of palmetto tree logs filled with sand in between, and when finished would hold approximately 1,000 soldiers and 300 pieces of artillery. However, by June 1776, only two sides had been finished, those on the southern and western sides.

In December 1775, Lord George Germain (the Secretary of State in Great Britain) decided he would send a British fleet to America to subdue the southern colonies. This fleet, under the command of Commodore Sir Peter Parker, would sail for Wilmington, North Carolina, where it would meet British Gen. Henry Clinton coming from Boston. The combined force would then proceed to either Virginia or South Carolina. Sailing with the British fleet to America was Clinton's new second in command, Maj. Gen. Charles Earl Cornwallis.

Clinton arrived off Cape Fear in North Carolina in February 1776, but by this point the situation had changed in the southern colonies. A small British detachment of soldiers was brutally repulsed at the battle of Great Bridge in Virginia on December 9, 1775, and later in February, American Patriots defeated a detachment of Loyalists at Moore's Creek Bridge in North Carolina.

Parker and Cornwallis arrived at Cape Fear in May. After hearing the news of Great Bridge and

John Rutledge was elected the President of South Carolina in 1776 and later the Governor of South Carolina. After the war, he was a delegate to the Constitutional Convention and after served on the Supreme Court. (nypl)

William Moultrie emerged during the Revolutionary War as one of South Carolina's greatest heroes. He was the colonel of the 2nd South Carolina regiment and later was promoted to the rank of general. Here he stands in his Continental uniform on Sullivan's Island with the flag he designed behind him. (nypl)

General Henry Clinton commanded the British army that joined Parker's fleet to Charleston in 1776. Clinton's and Parker's inability to properly coordinate an assault resulted in a disastrous campaign for the British. (nypl)

Moore's Creek Bridge, Parker and Clinton decided that instead of landing at North Carolina or heading to Virginia, they would set their sights on Charleston.

Parker and Clinton's forces arrived off the coast of Charleston Harbor on June 4, and "displayed 50 sail before the town," which panicked the citizens of the city. The British fleet consisted of 7 warships, more than 40 smaller vessels and transports, almost 300 cannon, and nearly 3,000 British soldiers. Moultrie later remembered: "Men [were] running about the town looking for horses, carriages, and boats to send their families into the country; and as they were going out . . . they met the militia from the country marching into town; traverses were made in the principal streets; fleches thrown up at every place where troops could land." Fear pervaded the city of Charleston.

As Moultrie remembered, the general opinion at this time was that "two frigates would be a sufficient force to knock the town about our ears." The soldiers and citizens made preparations for a fight.

On June 8, Continental Gen. Charles Lee arrived in Charleston, much to the relief of the increasingly apprehensive citizens. Lee was dispatched by Gen. George Washington to take command of the American troops there. Lee was born in England and previously had served in the British army and was universally thought of as one of the best military minds on the American side. Though he later proved to be a severe disappointment for the American cause, now he was regarded as a renowned military mastermind. Lee promised additional reinforcements of Virginia and North Carolina Continentals were on their way. Although Lee was "rough in his manners," Colonel Moultrie thought that his arrival and his reputation as an experienced soldier was "equal to a reinforcement of 1,000 men."

Lee immediately inspected the harbor's defenses and made numerous improvements. He was unimpressed with the unfinished fort on Sullivan's Island, which he called a "slaughter pen" and suggested that the fort be abandoned as there was no avenue of retreat for the garrison should it be attacked by Clinton's troops. Moultrie disagreed and argued that it be kept. Moultrie, meanwhile, was getting secret letters from John Rutledge that supported defending Sullivan's Island, even though publicly Rutledge proclaimed Lee as the commander of the harbor. This distrust of the Continental authority by the local authority foreshadowed future suspicions between the two throughout the war and after.

Lee demanded that at least a bridge of boats be built to connect Sullivan's Island to Haddrell's Point to save the garrison in the event of disaster. However, the Patriots didn't have enough boats to construct such a bridge, and Moultrie attempted to use hogshead barrels to create a floating bridge. But when they tried to use this span, it couldn't support the men trying to cross. Despite Lee's anxiety about the fort's defenders meeting disaster, Moultrie was unconcerned—he felt that his fort could stand up to the British fleet. He also planned to place American troops at the Breach Inlet to prevent a landing of British forces on the north end of Sullivan's Island.

Commodore Sir Peter Parker commanded the fleet that arrived in South Carolina in 1776. (nypl)

At one point, as it became clear the American troops on Sullivan's Island would not be able to retreat, Lee pulled Moultrie aside and asked, "Col. Moultrie, do you think you can maintain this post?" Moultrie responded: "Yes, I think I can." But Lee was not the only concerned military officer. A Patriot privateer, Capt. Clement Lamprière, inspected the works one day with Colonel Moultrie. Standing on top of the fort's walls, they looked at the British fleet, and Lamprière said, "when those ships (pointing to the men-of-war) come to lay along side of your fort, they will knock it down in half an hour." Moultrie coolly replied by saying that if that were to happen, "we will lay behind the ruins and prevent their men from landing." He and his men were willing to fight or die.

As the Patriots prepared for a defense, the British began to plan their attack. Parker decided that rather than avoiding the fort on Sullivan's Island, he would attack it head-on to open entry to the city. Clinton and Cornwallis had landed with about 2,000 British troops on an island just north of Sullivan's Island (Long Island, today Isle of Palms) on June 16. They were planning to launch a coordinated attack on the unfinished fort. The fleet would pound the palmetto log fort, while Clinton's men would cross over the Breach Inlet to Sullivan's Island and attack the fort on the ground. Clinton believed that "the Breach" (the small inlet of water between Sullivan's Island and Long Island) would be fordable at low tide, but he quickly discovered that this was not the case. The only way to affect a crossing would be by boat, and he didn't have enough boats to accomplish this mission.

General Charles Cornwallis's first action in South Carolina occurred at the Battle of Sullivan's Island. He went on to distinguish himself in other campaigns and returned to Charleston in 1780. (nypl)

Undeterred, Parker decided he would go it alone with the navy against the fort and left Clinton to do what he could to try and support the attack.

The fort on Sullivan's Island mounted only 31 cannon (ranging in size from 12 to 26 pounders) and 434 soldiers of the 2nd South Carolina Regiment. On the northern tip of Sullivan's Island at the Breach Inlet, Col. William "Danger" Thomson was posted with 780 men of the 3rd South Carolina Regiment and 4th South Carolina Artillery. They had two artillery pieces with them to defend any attempt by the British to advance across the Breach Inlet. Across the Cove at Haddrell's Point, Gen. Charles Lee and Gen. John Armstrong were stationed with reinforcements, a total of 1,500 men. Among these men were the 5th and 6th South Carolina Regiments, the 1st and 2nd North Carolina Regiments, and about 700 men of the 8th Virginia. The 8th Virginia was under the command of the famous preacher turned soldier, Col. Peter Muhlenberg.

The nine British ships mounted nearly 300 cannon ranging in size from 6 to 24 pounders. This strong fleet, part of one of the most powerful navies on the planet, had its sights set on a half-finished palmetto log fort. Sir Peter Parker on his flagship the *Bristol* along with the *Experiment* were the largest in the fleet with 50-guns. These ships, joined by the 28-gun *Active* and *Solebay*, would anchor just 400 yards from the palmetto log fort and pummel its front walls. As the large men-of-war battered the front walls of the fort, the *Thunder* (a bomb ship), joined by the 20-gun ship *Friendship*, would launch mortar shots over the wall and into the fort and inflict casualties on the defenders. Finally, the 28-gun ships *Acteon* and *Syren*, joined by the 20-gun *Sphinx*, would sweep wide around the southern tip of Sullivan's Island and flank the defenders. This position behind the fort would open the soft underbelly of the incomplete stronghold as well as prevent any attempt by the fort's defenders to escape. It appeared that the British had an insurmountable advantage in the coming action.

Parker ordered the assault to occur on June 23; however, the weather didn't cooperate, and the fleet waited for favorable winds to launch the assault. Meanwhile, Moultrie and his men used this extra time to further prepare for the assault. Both sides knew the attack could come at any moment and tension ran high in both military forces.

General Charles Lee was in overall command of the American troops at the Battle of Sullivan's Island. (nypl)

On the morning of June 28, 1776, Lee had grown impatient with Moultrie and ordered Col. Francis Nash of the North Carolina Continentals to relieve Moultrie of command. However, Nash was unable to get to Sullivan's Island before the soldiers saw the British sails rise and the ships begin sailing toward Sullivan's Island. The battle of Sullivan's Island was about to begin.

Honor and Victory: The Battle of Sullivan's Island

CHAPTER TWO

JUNE 28, 1776

"One continual blaze and roar"

— Colonel William Moultrie

A statue of William Moultrie dedicated in 2007 stands in White Point Garden on the Charleston Battery. He stares out in the direction of Sullivan's Island and the site of his most famous victory of the war. (mm)

At 11 a.m. on June 28, 1776, the nine British warships weighed anchor and began moving toward Sullivan's Island. At that moment, Colonel Moultrie was conferring with Col. William "Danger" Thomson, who commanded the 3rd South Carolina, which was placed at the northern end of the island near the Breach Inlet. When Moultrie heard the British fleet was advancing towards the fort, he quickly remounted his horse and rode there to take command. General Charles Lee tried to use a boat to get over to Sullivan's Island but was turned back by the waves and would have to watch the opening action from the rear at Haddrell's Point.

Moultrie ordered his men to their posts to prepare for the defense of the fort. At 11:30 a.m., the first shots of the battle were fired from the mortars on the *Thunder*. These mortar shells arced into the sky and came crashing down inside the fort's walls. The *Friendship* stayed with the *Thunder* and acted as her guard. Now the first four ships (*Bristol*, *Experiment*, *Solebay*, and *Active*) moved into position and anchored 400 yards from the fort. Moultrie's men returned fire at the *Active* as she dropped anchor and swung around to line up parallel with the walls of the fort before opening her cannon ports and rolling the artillery forward. Then in an amazing display of British firepower, *Active* fired a broadside, simultaneously firing all her cannon from one side of the ship. *Active*'s broadside was followed shortly by broadsides from the *Bristol*, *Experiment*,

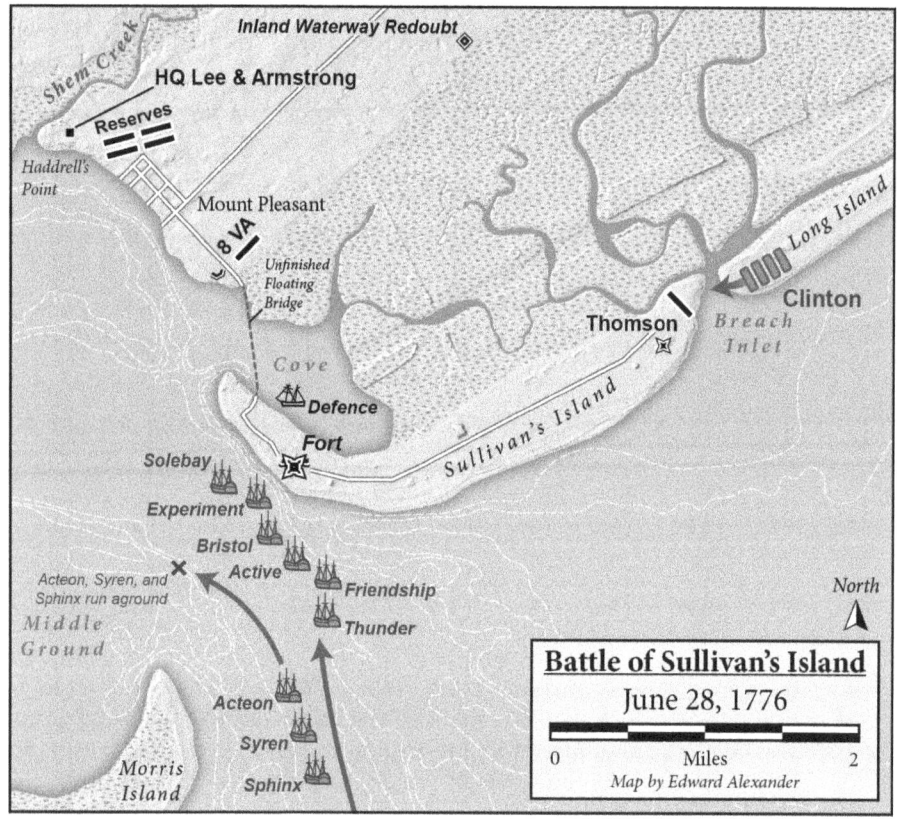

Battle of Sullivan's Island

June 28, 1776

0   Miles   2

Map by Edward Alexander

Battle of Sullivan's Island—**The British assault on the American position on Sullivan's Island came from the sea and from the land. Clinton's force was unable to get across the Breach Inlet and Parker's warships were driven back after trading artillery shots with the Americans all day.**

and the *Solebay*. The broadsides were deafening as hundreds of British cannonballs screeched through the air and slammed into the palmetto walls of the fort. Local newspapers later described the cannonade as "one of the most heavy and incessant cannonades perhaps ever known."

As these four ships engaged the unfinished fort, three more British ships (*Sphinx*, *Syren*, and *Acteon*) sailed up behind the front four.

As the walls of the fort shook violently, Moultrie's men coolly manned their cannon and returned the fire as best they could. A continuous roar of cannon fire from hundreds of artillery pieces belched forth, quickly filling the harbor with the sight of white smoke and the smell of burning sulfur. The crash of the cannonballs and the screams of wounded men filled the air.

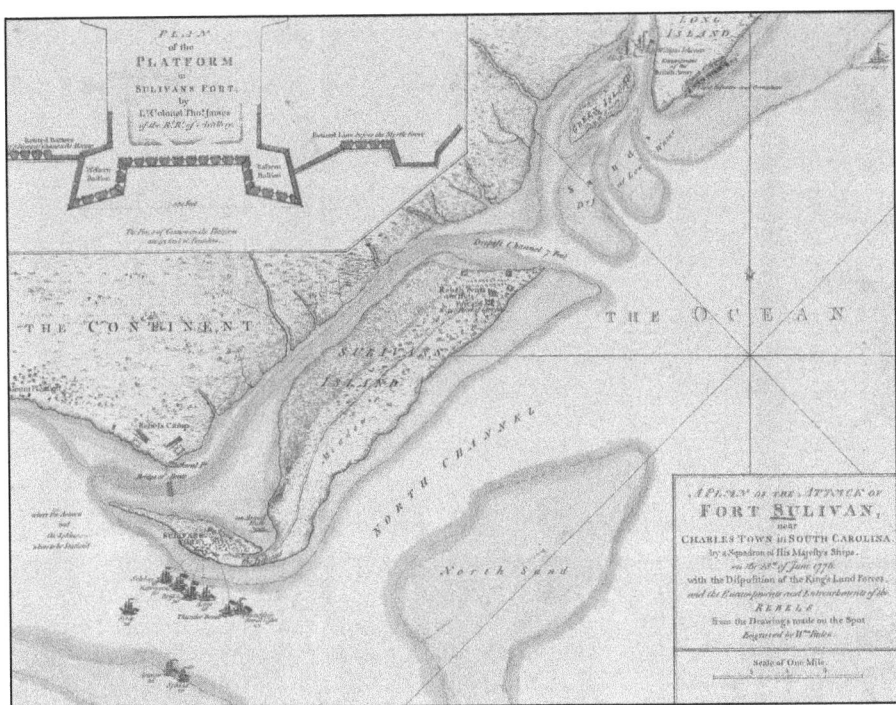

However, the British battle plan began to unravel almost from the beginning. As the *Thunder* continued to lob cannonballs over the walls of the fort, they soon began falling short. The ship had anchored about a mile and a half away, so the British captain ordered that more powder be used to launch the balls farther into the fort. This worked at first, but in the middle of the fort was a morass, and the cannonballs that landed in it were swallowed up by the sand and water and did not explode. Then, after about 60 shots, the overloaded artillery pieces strained under the massive amount of black powder, and the beds and deck the mortars were resting on broke. These guns were now incapacitated for the rest of the day's fight. To kill the defenders of the fort on Sullivan's Island, the British ships would need to blast down the walls.

Inside the fort, Moultrie directed his men to take particular aim at the two largest warships, the *Bristol* and *Experiment*, both carrying 50 guns. Despite the hurricane of violence bearing down on them, the men of the 2nd South Carolina manned their artillery pieces with efficiency and precision. Moultrie remembered once when three or four of the British broadsides hit the palmetto log walls at same time;

A British map of the battle that was drawn shortly after the action. (nypl)

Nothing remains of the original 1776 palmetto fort, but this 1809 brick fort is the third to be on this site. The 1776 fort was much larger than the current fort, though still unfinished during the battle. (mm)

the walls shook so violently that he thought they may come crumbling down. But they didn't.

Not very long into the battle it became clear that the Patriots, and not the powerful British navy, had the advantage in this struggle. As the British cannon boomed away, their solid shot would hit the walls of the palmetto fort. But the soft, spongy wood of the palmetto (and the 16 feet of sand behind them) absorbed the shock and the balls either buried themselves into the wall or bounced off and fell harmlessly to the ground. Meanwhile, the British ships endured terrible damage from the American shore batteries. American cannonballs smashed into the oak of the British ships, causing havoc and bloodshed.

A replica 18-pounder artillery piece sits outside of the 1809 Fort Moultrie near the site of the outer walls of the 1776 fort. (mm)

As Parker's front four ships continued to trade shots with Moultrie's men, the next three ships (*Acteon, Sphinx,* and *Syren*) started their planned movement around Sullivan's Island to fire into the unprotected rear of the fort. The three ships sailed to the south and west to make their way into "the Cove," the body of water that stood between Sullivan's Island and Haddrell's Point. However, the British pilots did not know the configuration of the harbor; thus, when they maneuvered toward the vulnerable rear, they ended up grounding on a shallow sand bar known as the "Middle Ground." It was on this same sandbar that Fort Sumter was built in the 19th century. All three ships became stuck on the sand and were now out of the battle. This costly error stole from the British their best option for driving Moultrie and his men from the fort.

As the British navy realized they were in for a long-drawn-out fight, the British army north of Sullivan's Island attempted to cross the Breach Inlet and land soldiers on Sullivan's Island. British soldiers piled onto small transport barges and began crossing the inlet. While some of Clinton's men were able to make it to the mainland to the west of Sullivan's Island, they received a heavy fire from Thomson's men, who unleashed volleys of musket and cannon fire on the British soldiers on the mainland and in the Breach. With no way to return cannon fire on the American position, the British soldiers in the Breach were sitting ducks. The barges were forced back and the British soldiers elected to fire at the Americans from across the inlet. Clinton attempted to cross multiple times but

A view from the tower in Fort Moultrie of where the 1776 battle occurred. The sidewalk on the outside of the walls of the 1809 fort gives a rough estimate of the approximate location of the palmetto walls of the 1776 fort. The British warships anchored 400 yards off the coast and traded shots with the American fort. On the right side of the image near the horizon you can see Fort Sumter, which did not exist in 1776, but three British warships ran aground on the sandbar at that location. (mm)

Inside Fort Moultrie today are reminders of more than 100 years of coastal defense from 1809 up until just after World War II. (mm)

View of the Charleston skyline from the beach at Fort Moultrie. Charlestonians watched the battle on June 28, 1776 from the city and kept close watch of the flag of the 2nd South Carolina flying above the fort. (mm)

was driven back by the spirited firing of Thomson's men, which continued for most of the afternoon. One Patriot remembered that the American artillery "spread Havock [sic], Devastation, and Death, and always made them retire faster than they advanced."

Later in the day, Thomson's 780 men were reinforced by more than 500 men from Col. Peter Mulhenberg's 8th Virginia Regiment. By blocking Clinton's advance, these soldiers ensured that the fort would not be taken.

Meanwhile, the battle continued to rage in front of the fort. Moultrie had his men focus most of their fire on the two largest ships, the *Experiment*, and Parker's flagship, the *Bristol*. At one point the spring line of the *Bristol* was hit and the ship drifted so that its aft was facing the fort. The cry rose up among the men "Mind the commodore, mind the two fifty gun

A large painting inside the Fort Moultrie Visitor Center depicts the violent action of June 28, 1776. (mm)

ships!" The Patriots poured a withering fire into the *Bristol*. Moultrie imagined that Parker "was not at all obliged to us, for our particular attention to him." A surgeon with the British fleet noted that the *Bristol* was "raked fore and aft" by American artillery. He wrote that "perhaps an instance of such slaughter cannot be produced; twice the quarter-deck was cleared of every person except Sir Peter." In the maelstrom on the *Bristol*, British officers and sailors quickly fell. The captain of the *Bristol*, John Morris, had his arm ripped off by an American cannonball and died a week later. The former royal governor of South Carolina, William Campbell, was also on board the *Bristol* and suffered a wound to his side and eventually died from it two years after the battle. Sir Peter Parker himself was wounded slightly in the fighting—his breeches were torn apart, and his thigh and knee were cut and bloody—and needed to be helped below deck. One British officer on the *Bristol* noted that "no slaughterhouse could present so bad a sight, with blood and entrails lying about, as our ship did."

A palmetto tree stands near the site of the 1776 palmetto log fort. The spongy wood of the palmetto helped to absorb the shock of British cannonballs on June 28, 1776. Ever since, it has been a symbol of South Carolina. (mm)

Meanwhile, in the fort, Moultrie's men coolly kept up their fire on the ships in a slow and deliberate manner. While the walls kept most of the garrison safe, British shots that made it through the embrasures killed and wounded some of Moultrie's men. The first man killed in the fort was Cpl. Samuel Yarbury. After he was hit and fell dead, the men pushed

A view of the Breach Inlet today from Sullivan's Island looking north to Long Island (modern day Isle of Palms). Col. William Thomson's successful defense of the British trying to cross over helped secure the American victory. (mm)

his body off the firing platform and yelled, "Revenge, let us revenge our comrade's death!" Not long after, Sgt. James McDaniel was hit by an enemy cannonball that took "off his shoulder and scouped [sic] out his stomach." While bleeding to death in the sand, McDaniel cried out: "Fight on, my brave boys; don't let liberty expire with me today!"

In perhaps the deadliest shot fired from the British fleet, a cannonball entered an embrasure and cut through the bodies of three men, killing them all. The three men: Luke Flood, Richard Rogers, and Isaac Edwards, fell without saying a word and only gasped a few times before they all died.

In other parts of the fort, limbs and lives were being lost as well. A British cannonball took off the head of John Boxall. Sergeant John Young had his leg torn away by a British cannonball but survived. One account noted that "several arms are shot away." The scene inside the fort became one of pandemonium, confusion, smoke, blood, and guts, yet the men continued to bravely do their duty regardless.

Chaos abounds in this depiction of the battle of Sullivan's Island. Men continue loading and firing artillery pieces at the British ships as casualties mount in the fort. (nypl)

At one point in the barrage, a British cannonball knocked the 2nd South Carolina's flag off the ramparts. In Charleston, hundreds of civilians looked on "with anxious hopes and fears, some of whom had their fathers, brothers, and husbands in the battle; whose hearts must have been pierced at every broadside." When they witnessed the flag struck, a gasp went

This print depicts the ferocious fighting that occurred all day on June 28, 1776, on Sullivan's Island. Notice Sergeant William Jasper raising the flag on the left side. (nypl)

up; they feared it was a sign that Moultrie was surrendering. Sergeant William Jasper, seeing the flag fall to the ground, yelled to Moultrie, "Don't let us fight without a flag!" Moultrie replied: "What can you do? The staff is broke." In a scene of amazing courage, Jasper jumped on top of the ramparts and ran down to the northeast bastion as cannonballs flew all around him. He jumped down to the outside of the fort and grabbed the blue flag. Climbing back up to the top of the rampart, he grabbed a sponge staff used by the artillerymen and fastened the banner to it. He then planted the makeshift flagpole into the rampart under a maelstrom of iron. Waving his hat, he exclaimed: "God save liberty and my country forever!" The flag securely in place, he jumped back safely into the fort. It was an amazing display of bravery under fire and "revived the drooping spirits" of the civilians in Charleston, prompting the men of the fort to break into loud cheers.

As the battle raged, General Lee sent Colonel Moultrie orders that if he ran out of gunpowder to spike the cannon, abandon the fort, and retreat to the mainland. Moultrie ordered his men to slow their fire and conserve the valuable powder.

Around three in the afternoon, as the firing raged at the Breach, Moultrie received the mistaken report that Clinton had been successful in overwhelming Thomson's men. Moultrie ordered his guns in the fort to stop firing entirely to preserve their limited powder supply. Parker and many in the British navy had optimistically thought this may have meant the defenders were surrendering. However, Parker did not attempt a landing and continued to pummel the fort.

In what became one of the most celebrated moments of the battle, Sergeant William Jasper courageously replaced the flag that had been shot away by a British cannonball. This moment was depicted repeatedly over the years, sometimes with inaccuracies, such as this print showing the soldiers wearing 19th century uniforms. (nypl)

Sergeant William Jasper's fame grew in the 19th century after Mason Locke Weems, the same man who wrote the famous George Washington biography with the stories of chopping down the cherry tree, wrote about Jasper's virtues and feats. (nypl)

The powder situation was becoming a serious issue for the Patriots. Moultrie began the day with 4,600 pounds of powder, and he was looking to conserve as much as possible to avoid a repeat of the situation at Bunker Hill, where the Patriots exhausted all their powder. At the beginning of the battle, Moultrie requested additional powder, and in the middle of the engagement, South Carolina President John Rutledge sent Moultrie 500 additional pounds from downtown Charleston with a note reading: "Honor and Victory, my good sir, to you, and our worthy countrymen with you. Do not make too free with your cannon. Cool and do mischief."

Among the officers serving in the fort under Moultrie that day was Maj. Francis Marion. Nicknamed "the Swamp Fox," Marion later earned fame in the war as a partisan fighter. At Sullivan's Island, he helped direct many of the cannon shots and at one point in the fighting left the fort to get 200 pounds of black powder that was sitting on a schooner (*Defence*) in the Cove behind the island.

Around 4 p.m., with the knowledge that Clinton had in fact been stopped from crossing the Breach Inlet, the Patriots resumed their destructive fire on the ships 400 yards off. Moultrie and his officers calmly smoked their pipes as the men labored in the heat. Moultrie recalled that they were served "grog [rum mixed with water] in fire-buckets, which we partook of very heartily: I never had a more agreeable draught than that which I took out of one of those buckets at the time."

Some of the men removed their blue wool coats because of the heat. At one moment a British cannonball sent one of the men's coats flying, which then got caught in a tree near the fort. Some British sailors mistakenly believed the coat was an American soldier who had been hanged for trying to desert.

Around this time, under heavy firing from the British, Gen. Charles Lee visited the fort from Haddrell's Point. He found the men in the fort "determined and cool to the last degree; their behaviour would, in fact, have done honour to the oldest troops." Lee even helped to aim a few cannon at the British fleet. He was supremely impressed with the conduct of Moultrie's men, describing the cannonade they endured as "the most furious and incessant fires I ever

Some depictions of the battle show the officers smoking their pipes, as Moultrie described in his memoirs. (nypl)

saw or heard." Lee was a veteran of numerous battles in the French and Indian War such as Braddock's Defeat and the battle of Carillon; thus, this was no small compliment. He noticed the dead and wounded in the fort and how many of the wounded were missing limbs. He then wrote, "with their limbs they did not lose their spirits; for they enthusiastically encouraged their comrades never to abandon the standard of liberty and their country. This I do assure you, is not the style of gasconading romance usual after every successful action but literally a fact."

William Jasper returns the flag to the parapet. (nypl)

Lee spent only a few minutes at the fort and said to Moultrie, "Colonel, I see you are doing very well here. You have no occasion for me. I will go up to town again."

With renewed vigor and more black powder, the Americans continued firing into the British ships. Later in the evening, two of the ships stuck in the "Middle Ground," the *Syren* and the *Sphinx*, were able to refloat as the tide came in. The *Syren* had to have her bowsprit cut off. The *Acteon*, though, was still firmly stuck on the sandbar.

The cannonading continued after the sun set and darkness fell. After more than 10 hours of furious cannonading, Parker reluctantly ordered his ships to retreat from the fort, and the proud British fleet limped away to lick its wounds. They suffered grievously in the fighting, both in damage to their ships and loss of lives and limbs. The *Bristol* suffered the most damage, having lost 40 men killed (including her captain) and 71 wounded (including the commodore). The *Experiment* suffered 23 killed and 56 wounded

Francis Marion was serving as a major in the fort on Sullivan's Island during the battle on June 28, 1776. (nypl)

An engraving of the British view of the island and fort during the battle. (nypl)

(including her captain). The *Active* suffered 1 killed and 6 wounded. The *Solebay* had 8 wounded. In total, 64 men were killed and 141 wounded. On the American side, Moultrie listed 12 men killed (including a slave who was referred to as a "mulatto waiting boy") and 25 men wounded. There were no recorded casualties at the Breach Inlet. It had been a long, hot, and bloody day, but the Americans successfully repelled the British invasion.

The next day, June 29, the captain of the *Acteon*, still stuck on the "Middle Ground," made the decision to abandon ship and scuttle her. In a scene of bravery and humor, after seeing the British set the ship on fire and leave, American soldiers under the command of Capt. Jacob Milligan quickly rowed out to the burning *Acteon*, hopped onboard and fired the cannon at the British fleet in the distance, then jumped ship before the fire reached the powder magazine. When that happened, the ship blew up in a huge explosion. Moultrie noted that the smoke cloud "formed the figure of a palmetto tree."

The Americans were victorious thanks to the brave defenders of the fort and the Breach, but also to the palmetto tree walls that had stood the bombardment so well. The following day, the Americans recovered hundreds of British cannonballs that had hit the walls and either embedded themselves or bounced off. Because of the victory at the battle of Sullivan's Island,

An engraving of the British view of the harbor on the day after the battle. Notice the burning *Acteon* that was abandoned by the British. (nypl)

the palmetto tree became the state's symbol and can be seen emblazoned on the state flag to this day. Also, the state seal of South Carolina portrays the palmetto tree over a broken oak tree. The oak tree represents the British navy, as their ships were made of oak, and the palmetto represents the fort on Sullivan's Island.

Moultrie never forgot the men who fought and died that day. In his memoirs, written more than 25 years later, he remembered that "never did men fight more bravely, and never were men more cool." He wrote to be in the fort that day was "a very honorable situation, but a very unpleasant one."

The day had been a glorious one for the South Carolinians. A few days after the battle, Sergeant Jasper was given a sword by President Rutledge for his bravery in repairing the colors in the middle of the fight. He was offered a promotion due to his gallantry but refused it to continue serving as a sergeant in the 2nd South Carolina. The regiment was given two new regimental flags by Susannah Elliott, the wife of Maj. Barnard Elliott. One was red and one was blue, with a crest on them and the Latin motto: "Vita Potior Libertas" or "Liberty rather than life." She presented them to Moultrie and Marion with the words: "Your gallant behavior in defence of liberty and your country, entitles you to the highest honors; accept these two standards as a reward justly due to your regiment; and I make not the least doubt, under Heaven's protection, you will stand by them as long as they can wave

One of the defenders of the fort who was wounded on June 28, 1776, was Lt. Henry Gray. After the battle, he painted this image of the battle. An amazing depiction made by an actual participant. (loc)

The British abandoning the *Acteon* after she ran aground on "The Middle Ground." (nypl)

The sandbar where the *Acteon* ran aground is today the site of Fort Sumter. Begun in 1829, Fort Sumter was named for General Thomas Sumter, a hero of the Revolutionary War. It became the target at which the first shots of the Civil War were fired in 1861. (mm)

in the air of liberty." Three years later at Savannah in 1779, Sergeant Jasper risked his life carrying one of these flags, but was not as lucky as he was at Sullivan's Island.

Other 2nd South Carolina officers who distinguished themselves that day received honors, including Major Marion, who earned a promotion to lieutenant colonel. Moultrie was made a brigadier general in the Continental Army.

The news of the day's battle was received throughout America as a great victory. Lee wrote to General Washington and John Hancock, the president of the Continental Congress, about the astounding success. News of the great victory arrived in Philadelphia on July 20, 1776, a little more than two weeks after Congress had voted to declare independence from Great Britain. John Adams noted that "it has given us good Spirits here and will have an happy Effect, upon our Armies at New York and

The state flag of South Carolina enshrines the significance of the battle of Sullivan's Island in the symbolism of the crescent and palmetto tree. (wiki)

Ticonderoga. Surely our northern Soldiers will not suffer themselves to be outdone by their Brethren."

On July 21, General George Washington issued his general orders for the Continental army and relayed to the troops "the signal success of the American Arms" at Sullivan's Island. Washington noted that "The Firmness, Courage and Bravery of our Troops, has crowned them with immediate Honor. The dying Heroes conjured their Brethren never to abandon the Standard of Liberty, and even those who had lost their Limbs, continued at their posts: Their Gallantry and Spirit extorted applause from their enemies, who dejected & defeated, have retired to their former station, out of the reach of our troops." Washington hoped this example would inspire the army he commanded and wrote: "With such a bright example before us, of what can be done by brave and spirited men, fighting in defense of their Country; we shall be loaded with a double share of Shame, and Infamy, if we do not acquit ourselves with Courage, or a determined Resolution to conquer or die." This was high praise from the commander in chief of the Continental army.

The state seal of South Carolina depicts the palmetto tree over a fallen oak tree. (sc)

Just a few weeks later, on August 12, Charlestonians learned that on July 4, 1776, the Continental Congress had declared independence, and celebrations were held throughout the city. While July 4 would be a revered day for independence, the people never forgot the victory on June 28. The day would be termed "Palmetto Day" or "Carolina Day," and every year after (from 1777 through today) the people of Charleston and South Carolina celebrate the June 28 victory over the British invaders.

Driving Tour 1

This tour will focus on the sites associated with the June 28, 1776, battle of Sullivan's Island. It starts at Fort Moultrie on Sullivan's Island and ends in downtown Charleston.

GPS: N 32.759263, W 79.857736

A reproduction artillery piece on the site where the battle of Sullivan's Island occurred on June 28, 1776. (mm)

Tour Stop 1 — Fort Moultrie

As storms battered the remnants and the old palmetto logs rotted, in 1798, a new Fort Moultrie was built on the ruins of the first. However, in 1804 this new fort was destroyed by a hurricane. The structure you see today was built in 1809. It served as the primary defensive fortification for Charleston until 1829 when construction on Fort Sumter began on the "Middle Ground," where the *Acteon* had grounded. In 1860, Maj. Robert Anderson and the United States soldiers guarding Charleston Harbor were stationed at Fort Moultrie when South Carolina seceded from the Union. A few days later, he moved his men over to Fort Sumter. Some of the first shots of the American Civil War were fired at Fort Sumter by South Carolina soldiers from Fort Moultrie. Moultrie continued to be used as a coastal defense fort up until and after World War II before being transferred in 1947 to the National Park Service.

Today inside the Fort Moultrie Visitor Center is a museum that interprets the history of Fort Moultrie from 1776 to 1947. (mm)

While the 1776 fort no longer exists, the sidewalk around the fort gives a general idea of the palmetto fort's size. You can also see replica artillery like ones used by Moultrie's men. Because the shifting sands of Charleston Harbor have added more land to the island, the water line in 1776 was closer to the fort.

The National Park Service interprets this battle on-site today. A museum offers insights into not only the 1776 battle, but also the Civil War and almost 200-year coastal defense of Charleston Harbor.

> 1214 Middle St.
> Sullivan's Island, SC 29482
> GPS: N 32.759263, W 79.857736

➤ TO TOUR STOP 2

Before leaving the Fort Moultrie site, head to the northern part of the parking lot. In the field next to the water is a small black iron fence surrounding a gravestone. This is the grave of William Moultrie.

> GPS: N 32.762373, W 79.857023

William Moultrie was promoted to brigadier general after the battle at Sullivan's Island, and the fort was renamed in his honor. He took part in battles at Savannah and at Charleston in 1780, and in 1782 was made a major general. After the war, he served two terms as governor of South Carolina and wrote memoirs about the Revolutionary War. He died in 1805 at his home, Windsor Hill plantation, and was buried there. He was moved to this spot in 1978.

> 1214 Middle St., Sullivan's Island, SC 29482
> GPS: N 32.762373, W 79.857023

➤ TO TOUR STOP 3

Leave the Fort Moultrie parking lot and turn left onto Middle St. Stay on Middle St. for 2.8 miles, passing through the small village on Sullivan's Island. Before you arrive at Jasper Blvd., turn right into the small parking lot at Thomson Park.

> GPS: N 32.774858, W 79.814726

William Moultrie's body now lies just a few hundred feet from his greatest military victory of the Revolutionary War. A reproduction flag that flew at the battle flies over his grave. The inscription on his tombstone relates how he refused British efforts to persuade him to defect to the British cause. Moultrie was determined to act as a "man of honor." (mm)

Tour Stop 3 — Thomson Park

This is the area known as the Breach Inlet, where Col. William "Danger" Thomson and South Carolina, North Carolina, and Virginia troops prevented the soldiers of Gens. Henry Clinton and Charles Cornwallis from crossing the Long Island (Isle of Palms). Today a history park interprets the story of the fight at the Breach Inlet with historical interpretive markers. The inlet has changed over the years, but you still get a good sense of what the British soldiers were up against in June 1776. This was also the location where in February 1864 the Confederate submarine CSS *Hunley* (the first submarine to sink an enemy ship) set off to never return.

3217 Middle St., Sullivan's Island, SC 29482
GPS: N 32.774858, W 79.814726

⟫ TO TOUR STOP 4

Turn right out of the parking lot onto Middle St. Take a left at the stop sign onto Jasper Blvd. Follow Jasper Blvd for 1.5 miles and turn right onto Station 22½ St. (SC-703). Stay on SC-703 for 1.9 miles, crossing over onto the mainland. Turn left onto Center St and follow it for 1.2 miles. Turn left onto Pitt St. and follow to near the end in 0.4 miles. Park along the road, and if you would like, you can walk 0.3 miles out onto the Pitt St. Bridge.

GPS: N 40.295556, W 74.946944

Created in 2011, Thomson Park is a great spot to learn about the action that occurred on the north side of the island. Interpretive panels include maps and illustrations detailing the fighting there on June 28, 1776. (mm)

Tour Stop 4 — The Cove

This is the location of the body of water behind Sullivan's Island. It was across this water that General Lee wanted to build a bridge and where he crossed to get to the fort during the battle. This was also the location the three British ships (*Acteon*, *Sphinx*, and *Syren*) were trying to reach to bombard the fort from its unprotected rear but instead ran aground on the "Middle Ground."

▶ TO TOUR STOP 5

Turn around and head back out Pitt St. Stay on Pitt St. for 1.2 miles. Turn right onto Morrison St. and then make your first left onto Whilden St. Stay on Whilden St. for 0.3 miles and turn left onto Live Oak Dr. After 0.1 miles, turn right to stay on Live Oak Dr. In 0.2 miles, you will see a historic marker near the stop sign.

GPS: N 32.789177, W 79.883225

Along the Pitt Street bridge is a historic marker for the Cove Inlet. In the distance is the lighthouse on Sullivan's Island. (mm)

Tour Stop 5 — Haddrell's Point

This is the location of Haddrell's Point, off Shem Creek. It was at this location that Gen. James Armstrong and Gen. Charles Lee had their headquarters during the battle. This is also the general area where many of the North Carolina and Virginia Continentals were held in reserve during the battle.

203 Haddrell St., Mt Pleasant, SC 29464
GPS: N 32.789177, W 79.883225

➡ TO TOUR STOP 6

Today at the site of Haddrell's Point a historic marker denotes the Revolutionary War importance of the location. (mm)

Turn right onto Haddrell St. and go 0.1 miles. Turn right onto Magwood Ln. and go 260 feet. Turn left onto Live Oak Dr. and go 170 feet. Turn left to stay on Live Oak Dr. for 0.1 miles. Turn left at the 2nd cross street onto Whilden St. and then merge onto Coleman Blvd. Follow Coleman Blvd., US-17 S, for 4 miles over the Arthur Ravenel, Jr. Bridge. Use the right lane to take the Morrison Dr. ramp to E. Bay St. Use any lane to turn left onto Morrison Dr. Stay on Morrison Dr. as it turns into E. Bay St. Stay on E. Bay St. for 2.5 miles.

GPS: N 32.769674, W 79.928771

Tour Stop 6 — The Battery

This is the location of the Battery in downtown Charleston. The park here is called White Point Garden. Here you will see some of the finest private homes in Charleston, as well as numerous monuments

The base of the monument includes a quote from General Charles Lee. (mm)

and markers. We will focus on two monuments in particular. Looking out to the harbor and Sullivan's Island is a statue of William Moultrie that was erected in 2007. Behind him you will see a monument for the 2nd South Carolina Regiment with a statue of Sgt. William Jasper holding the flag on top. This statue was erected in 1876 on the centennial of the battle of Sullivan's Island. Today, it is the location of the annual commemoration of the battle.

2 Murray Blvd.
Charleston, SC 29401
GPS: N 32.769674, W 79.928771

(ABOVE) The monument down at White Point Garden to the defenders of Sullivan's Island is topped by a statue of Sgt. William Jasper holding the flag. The uniform he wears is a 19th century uniform and surrounding the base are quotes, bas reliefs, and a list of all those killed and wounded in the battle. (mm)

A bas relief depicts Sgt. Jasper placing the flag on the ramparts of the fort. (mm)

Quiet Harbor, Charleston

CHAPTER THREE

1776–1778

"I have the happiness to congratulate You on a very signal success (if I may not call it a victory) which We have gain'd over the mercenary Instruments of the British Tyrant."

— Gen. Charles Lee to Gen. George Washington, July 1, 1776

As Parker's fleet retreated out of Charleston Harbor and to the other side of the bar, the people of Charleston breathed a collective sigh of relief. Parker believed his men had fought in a "truly British spirit," but it was not enough to win the day. General Henry Clinton's men stayed on Long Island for almost two weeks before boarding transports to rejoin the British fleet. During that time the redcoats despised being stuck on an island in summer that "harbor[ed] millions of musketoes, a greater plague than can be hell itself." By the end of July, the British ships had left Charleston's waters, with some of the fleet heading south to the West Indies to be repaired and resupplied, and others sailing north to reinforce Gen. William Howe's army concentrating in New York City.

The British were stunned by the loss, and Parker and Clinton immediately began a war of words over who was to blame. Parker seemed to insinuate that Clinton's failure to cross the Breach Inlet was the cause for defeat, but Parker had clearly refused to work closely with the British infantry in effecting a landing. In four years, Clinton would return to Charleston, but this time as commander in chief of all British forces.

The Old Sheldon Church ruins just outside of Beaufort, South Carolina, were ravaged by multiple wars. They were first burned by the British in 1779 and then burned again by Union troops in 1865. (mm)

But for at least the next two years, Charleston did not see any British troops as the main theater of action moved back to the northern and mid-Atlantic states. Immediately after the victory at Sullivan's Island, Gen. Charles Lee and the Continentals went on an

Charleston as it appeared during the Revolutionary War. Note the defensive wall along the city. The city had a defensive wall built in the early 1700s to protect against foreign invaders. The harborside walls were reinforced during the Revolutionary War. Today, portions of the colonial wall continue to be discovered by archaeologists and plaques mark some of the locations of the old walled city. (nypl)

expedition down towards British East Florida before being called back to the main army in New Jersey. Charleston Harbor was quiet for a while and the city continued trading, bringing in much needed supplies and money to support the war effort in the north.

In 1777 and 1778, Charlestonians celebrated the June 28 victory over the British with parades, feasts, cannon salutes, drinking, toasts, and fireworks. Moultrie, Lee, and Jasper were honored along with George Washington and every man who gave his life in defense of the city.

While South Carolina enjoyed a reprieve from action, Gen. George Washington and his army met near-total defeat and capture in New York and New Jersey. In this campaign, Gen. Charles Lee was taken prisoner by British cavalry. But then Washington turned the tide with stunning victories at Trenton and Princeton in late 1776 and early 1777 that rallied his Patriots to keep up the fight. In the summer of 1777, the British set their sights on the United States capital at Philadelphia, and, after defeating the Continental army at Brandywine, they captured the seat of the American government. An American attempt to retake the capital failed at the battle of Germantown in October 1777.

But that same month, an army commanded by Gen. Horatio Gates defeated a British army under the command of Gen. John Burgoyne near Saratoga, New York. That victory helped the United States secure a formal treaty with France in 1778. This made the American rebellion a global conflict, which changed British strategy for the remainder of the war. With resources now needed to fight the French around the world and their Caribbean possessions threatened, the British decided to settle for a stalemate in the northern theater and to shift their emphasis to the south, where it was thought many Loyalists would flock to serve the King and perhaps bear much of the burden of fighting.

While George Washington was focused on the main British army at New York City, he understood the precarious situation in the South and helped to support the American efforts in that theatre. (mma)

With the British shift in strategy due to France's intervention, in the summer of 1778 Clinton (now commander in chief of British forces in North America) and the British army evacuated Philadelphia and returned to New York City. On the way, his army fought Washington and Lee (who had recently been exchanged) to a stalemate at the battle of Monmouth before falling back to New York. At this battle, Lee's reputation was destroyed after he ordered his men to fall back in the opening stages of the fighting. He was later court-martialed and cashiered from the army, leaving Washington more secure in his position as the commander in chief of the Continental army. By the end of 1778, the British were sailing for Georgia where they captured the port city of Savannah. In 1779, they began to work their way back to South Carolina.

To confront this growing threat, Washington sent a new general to command the Continental army's southern department in Charleston. That general was Benjamin Lincoln. Lincoln was originally from Massachusetts and fought with distinction at the beginning of the war. At the battle of Saratoga, he was shot in the ankle by a British musket ball that would cause him to walk with a limp for the rest of his life. Lincoln arrived in Charleston late in 1778 and soon consolidated his forces along the Savannah River to prevent an invasion of the Carolinas.

With a firm hold on Savannah, the British began sending expeditions into the countryside to put down the rebels and hopefully excite the supposed Loyalists in the area. These expeditions resulted in engagements at Brier Creek and Kettle Creek. But despite the presence of British soldiers, no large Loyalist uprising emerged. In February 1779, a British detachment was

Benjamin Lincoln was appointed to command the Southern department of the Continental army in 1778. (nypl)

sent to Beaufort, South Carolina, just 35 miles south of Charleston. In response, Gen. William Moultrie with some Continentals and militia rushed to oppose them. A small skirmish was fought, and the British detachment was driven back.

In April 1779, General Lincoln decided to move most of his army from Charleston west to Augusta, Georgia, to quell any possible Loyalist uprisings in the area. He left behind Moultrie with just 220 Continentals and 1,000 militia to hold off any attempt by the British to move north from Savannah. Moultrie positioned his force on the Savannah River to keep an eye on the British.

At the end of April, while Lincoln was away, British Gen. Augustine Prevost moved an army across the Savannah River and invaded South Carolina. Moultrie immediately had his small force fall back towards Beaufort and requested that Lincoln return to Charleston immediately. Moultrie moved his 1,200 men across the Coosawhatchie River and prepared to make a defense against Prevost's 2,400-man army. Moultrie realized, though, that the Coosawhatchie was not a strategically viable place to make a defense and instead moved across the Tulifiny River, leaving just 100 men at the Coosawhatchie. On May 3, 1779, Prevost's men arrived at the Coosawhatchie. Moultrie dispatched a young Lt. Col. John Laurens to take 250 men and retrieve the 100-man guard at the bridge there. But instead of escorting the guard back to the Tulifiny, Laurens, hot headed and eager to fight, took his 350-man detachment and assaulted Prevost's army. The British took cover near some farmhouses and poured volleys of musket balls into the small cluster of men. After taking about a dozen casualties, including Laurens, who was wounded, the men fell back to Moultrie's camp.

Unfortunately, this brief but deadly skirmish was a common issue for the young 24-year-old lieutenant colonel. Laurens was originally from Charleston, South Carolina, and his father was Henry Laurens, who had served as the president of the Continental Congress. John Laurens was studying the law in England when the Revolutionary War broke out, and in December 1776, he returned to America and immediately joined the Continental Army. Laurens was made an aide-de-camp to General Washington and became good friends with the Marquis de Lafayette and Alexander Hamilton. He fought bravely

British General Augustine Prevost commanded an army that invaded South Carolina in 1779. (nypl)

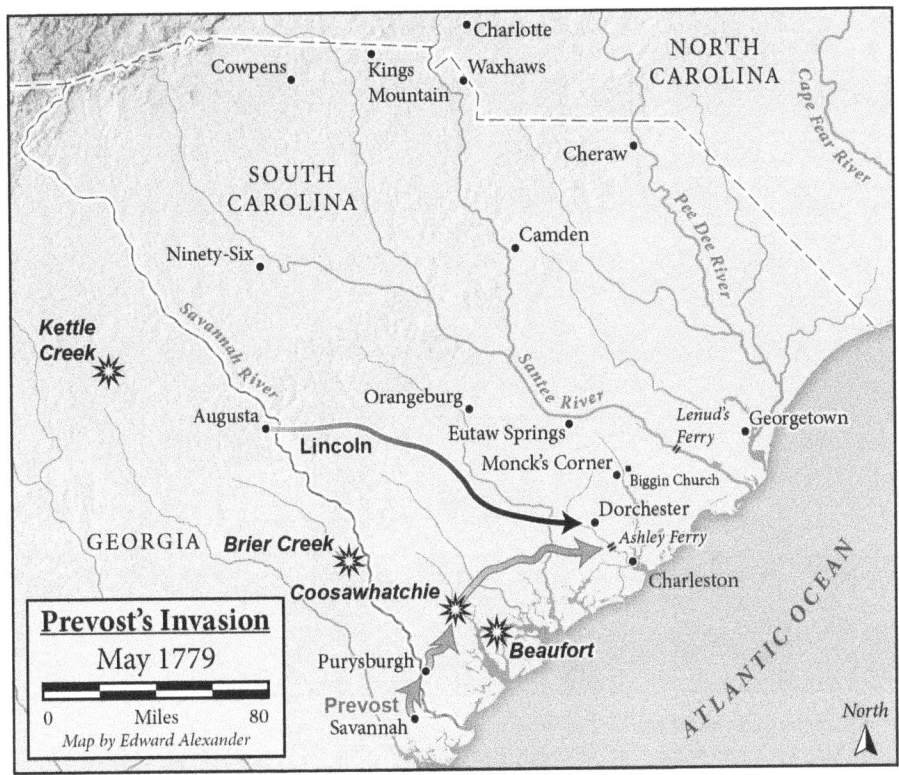

PREVOST'S INVASION—In 1779, following skirmishes at Beaufort, Kettle Creek, and Brier Creek, Gen. Augustine Prevost launched an invasion of South Carolina to threaten Charleston. Gen. William Moultrie fell back to the city to defend and waited for relief from Gen. Benjamin Lincoln who was returning from Augusta.

by Washington's side at the battles of Brandywine and Germantown, and at the latter was wounded in the assault on the Chew house. Laurens served through the winter at Valley Forge and fought again with Washington at the battle of Monmouth. Following that battle, Laurens fought a duel with Charles Lee after Lee had disparaged Washington, which resulted in Lee being wounded. Though he was raised in a large slave-holding family, Laurens was anti-slavery and hoped the institution would be destroyed. He advocated raising a regiment of bondsmen to defend the United States, but his suggestion was denied by the South Carolina government, which was uneasy with the idea of arming slaves. Laurens returned to South Carolina in April 1779 and joined Moultrie's army just prior to the skirmish at the Coosawhatchie. While Moultrie was upset at Laurens's reckless assault,

A view of the Coosawhatchie River from the south bank looking north. Lt. Col. John Laurens and his small American force crossed near here and attacked the British army. After a brief fight, the Americans fell back towards Charleston. (mm)

John Laurens was a young and passionate fighter for American independence but had a proclivity for rash and impulsive acts. (nypl)

his behavior eventually proved to be a deadly issue for Laurens.

With Prevost quick on his heels, Moultrie decided he needed to fall back all the way to Charleston. His numbers quickly dwindled, though, as many men deserted and went home to defend their properties from the vandalism of the British, who looted and destroyed much that was in their path. Moultrie repeatedly begged Lincoln to send reinforcements from Augusta, but Lincoln sent very few. Moultrie wrote that "I fear the town is in danger" and that "the enemy carry everything before them with fire and sword."

As Prevost continued toward Charleston, by May 8 Lincoln and his army finally turned around and headed to its relief. Moultrie remembered "nothing but general confusion and alarm" throughout this part of South Carolina. His army had been reduced by half; only 600 men were with him when he crossed the Ashley River at Dorchester (18 miles from the city). On May 9, he marched into Charleston.

Once back at Charleston, Moultrie immediately began building earthwork fortifications on the Charleston Neck. While the harbor had been well fortified, its land side had not and required quick work to put up a defense there. Meanwhile, on May 10, Prevost captured boats at Ashley Ferry, just seven miles from Charleston. The next day, the British with 900 men crossed the Ashley River and began descending on the capital of South Carolina. With Lincoln still miles away, Prevost was set to pounce on the lightly defended city.

Henry Laurens was one of the wealthiest planters in the Lowcountry. He served as the President of the Continental Congress in 1777 and 1778. (nypl)

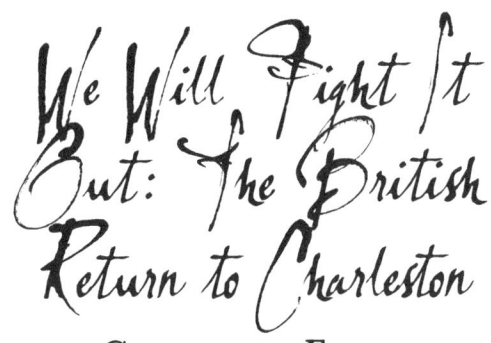

We Will Fight It Out: The British Return to Charleston

CHAPTER FOUR

1779

"The enemy carry everything before them with fire and sword."
— Gen. William Moultrie to
Gen. Benjamin Lincoln, 1779

Sergeant William Jasper and American soldiers endure a hail of shot as they place the American colors on the top of Spring Hill Redoubt in Savannah, Georgia, on October 9, 1779. Jasper fell in the effort and became a martyr in the cause for independence. (loc)

On May 8, the day before Moultrie's men entered Charleston, a mixed American force of 120 men—60 infantry and 60 cavalry—under the command of a Polish nobleman named Casimir Pulaski, arrived at Haddrell's Point from the north. Born in Poland and a veteran of battles in Europe, Pulaski came to America to join in the fight for liberty. Pulaski distinguished himself at the battle of Brandywine and was made a brigadier general in the Continental army. He became known as the "Father of the American Cavalry." In 1778, he created a legion made up of light infantry and cavalry. This unit, known as Pulaski's Legion or the American Legion, was composed largely of British and Hessian deserters. On May 11, they crossed the Cooper River and entered the fortifications of Charleston.

Seeing that there was a vanguard of British soldiers moving towards the American fortifications, Pulaski's men moved out of the entrenchments and engaged the British on the grounds of the New Market horse racetrack. Pulaski's men fought bravely but were outnumbered and quickly overwhelmed. While the mounted cavalrymen engaged the British dragoons, Pulaski's infantry took heavy casualties. After a brief and bloody fight, his men fell back into the town's fortifications. Nearly all the infantry were killed, wounded, or captured.

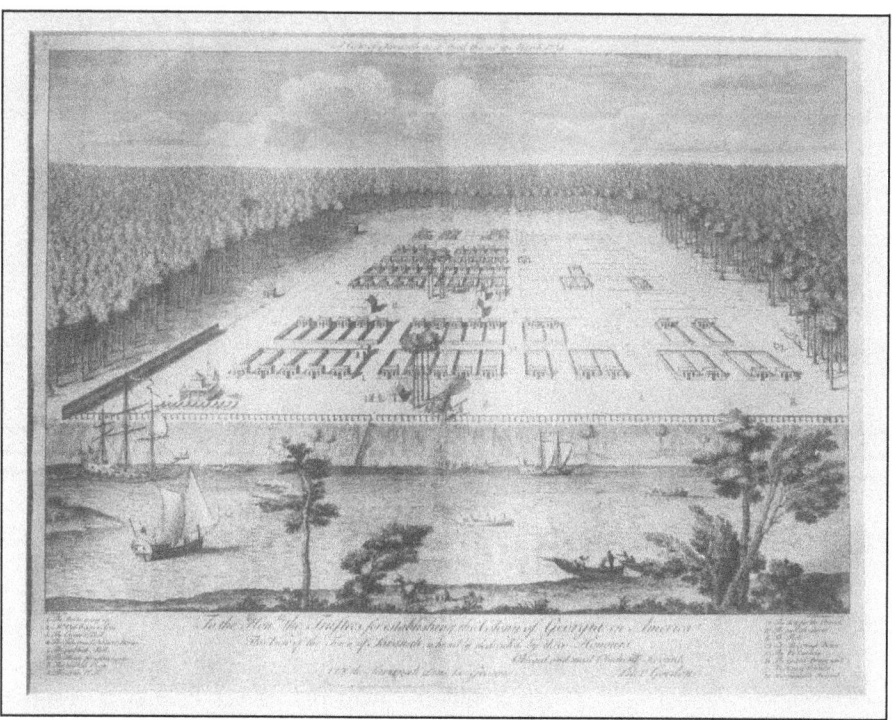

The city of Savannah, Georgia, is the oldest city in Georgia, founded in 1733. The city was originally laid out with multiple city squares. These squares have expanded and today, visitors can wander the numerous open squares throughout the city. (nypl)

The British vanguard advanced to within a mile of the city's defenses but was halted by artillery fire from the American defenses.

Later that night, a detachment of American soldiers left the lines to repair some of the abatis in front of the works. On their way back, they were mistaken for the enemy and their friends opened fire on them, resulting in 13 Americans killed and wounded. Among the dead was Maj. Benjamin Huger, a good friend of the Marquis de Lafayette.

In the early morning hours of May 12, Governor John Rutledge met with General Moultrie and requested that they parley with the British for terms to avoid the impending assault. Moultrie was against negotiating a surrender, but he deferred to Rutledge's civil authority. A message was sent to the British under a flag of truce requesting their terms. The reply came around 11 a.m., and it was chilling.

The British noted that they would provide "peace and protection" to the people of Charleston who accepted it, but all others would be made prisoners of war. However, if these terms were refused, "the evils and horrors attending the event of a storm" would be thrust upon the people of Charleston. The British gave the Patriots four hours to decide.

Rutledge convened his Privy Council and invited Moultrie to join them at his home on Broad Street. Moultrie brought Pulaski and Laurens with him. Rutledge and most of the Council did not think that the city could be defended from an assault, but Moultrie, Pulaski, and Laurens disagreed and argued that they should not give up the town without a fight. What followed was highly controversial. Rutledge offered that if the British agreed not to assault the city, South Carolina would declare itself neutral for the remainder of the war. This was a shocking proposition, and, in many ways, was a rejection of the American union and a betrayal of the cause of independence. But Rutledge and many South Carolinians felt that the Continental Congress had abandoned them and had not provided necessary aid and support. Rutledge and the majority of the Privy Council believed they were looking out for their best interests and safety.

However, many Charlestonians, including three members of the Privy Council, thoroughly rejected this idea. Among those opposed were Christopher Gadsden, former commander of South Carolina state forces, lieutenant governor, and the designer of the "Don't Tread on Me" Gadsden flag, and John Edwards, another leading local politician. Gadsden was furious, and Edwards was moved to tears. Moultrie and the Continentals were very

Col. Casmir Pulaski would go on to be remembered as a great Polish hero of the American Revolution. (nypl)

The John Rutledge House was completed in 1763. Though the ironwork was added in the 19th century, it was in this home where John Rutledge held a council of war in 1779. George Washington breakfasted here in 1791 and today it is operated as a bed and breakfast. (mm)

Christopher Gadsden was a staunch supporter of American independence and argued against offering terms to the British. (nypl)

much against the proposal, which would make them prisoners if it was accepted. They maintained they could and should defend the city, and they refused to be part of any deal with the British. Rutledge, thinking the British had as many as three times the number of troops they had, could not be convinced that he should subject the city to an assault, and he sent the British the controversial proposal. The British however rejected it out of hand; Prevost determined he did not have the authority to negotiate such a deal. Moultrie was relieved and exclaimed to the governor and the Council that "we will fight it out!" and retired to prepare his Continentals for the frontal assault he expected on their lines the next day.

However, on the morning of May 13, they discovered to their amazement that the British were gone. With news that Lincoln's army was quickly advancing towards Charleston, Prevost did not want his small force caught between Lincoln's and Moultrie's armies. Prevost's force retreated across the Ashley River and headed south toward Savannah. But Prevost considered it a success that he had traversed the state and threatened the South Carolina capital with such a small force, and, maybe more importantly, had struck fear in the hearts of the Patriots of the state and left state leaders contemplating leaving the fight altogether. But in his swath of destruction, he had alienated many of the Loyalists in the region, and his retreat disheartened many others. For the second time, Charleston had survived a British invasion. Granted, this was more of a raid, and no major combat took place other than the brief fighting with Pulaski's Legion on May 11.

As the British raiding army fell back, Prevost left a rearguard force of about 800 troops under the command of Lieut. Col. John Maitland at the Stono Ferry near Johns Island. Here, the Stono River divided Johns Island from the mainland. General Lincoln's army had shadowed the British through their retreat, and while there was some minor skirmishing, Lincoln was looking for an opportunity to strike a heavy blow. With enlistments set to expire for

THE GADSDEN FLAG OF 1776.

Christopher Gadsden designed the popular flag with a rattlesnake and the words "Don't Tread on Me." (nypl)

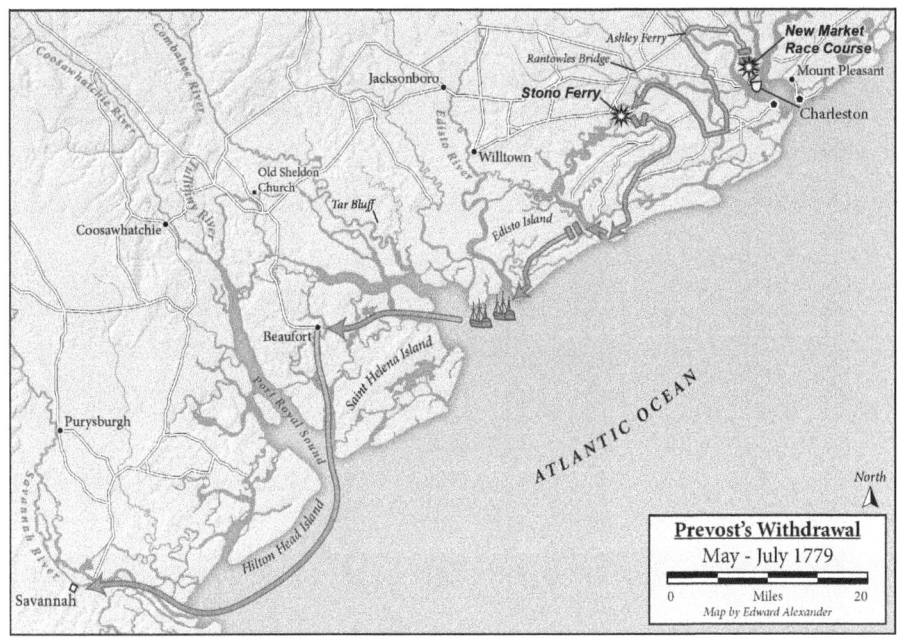

PREVOST'S WITHDRAWAL—**After fighting briefly outside the walls of Charleston, Prevost withdrew back to British occupied Savannah, Georgia. Along the way, a rear guard action was fought at Stono Ferry on June 20, 1779.**

many of his men, he thought a decisive attack would revive the drooping morale of the Continentals.

On June 19, the Patriots received word that the 800 men at Stono Ferry were about to retreat. Lincoln decided it was time to strike, and on June 20, 1779, he led a force of 3,000 men in an attack on the British soldiers there. The British were entrenched with the river to their back, and when firing commenced in some woods near their lines, Lieutenant Colonel Maitland dispatched two companies of the 71st Regiment of Foot to drive out what he assumed was a raiding party. Instead, they ran headlong into South Carolina Continentals and suffered heavy casualties. The remaining redcoats fell back into their works with the Continentals following closely. The Continentals made it to within 60 yards of Maitland's retreating men when the main British line opened fire on them. Stunned, the Continentals halted and returned fire. The opposing sides blasted musketry into each other for nearly thirty minutes. As the Continentals exchanged volleys with the 71st Regiment on the British right flank, Gen. Jethro Sumner and South Carolina militia furiously attacked the Hessians and Loyalists guarding the British left. The Hessians, surprised at the ferocity

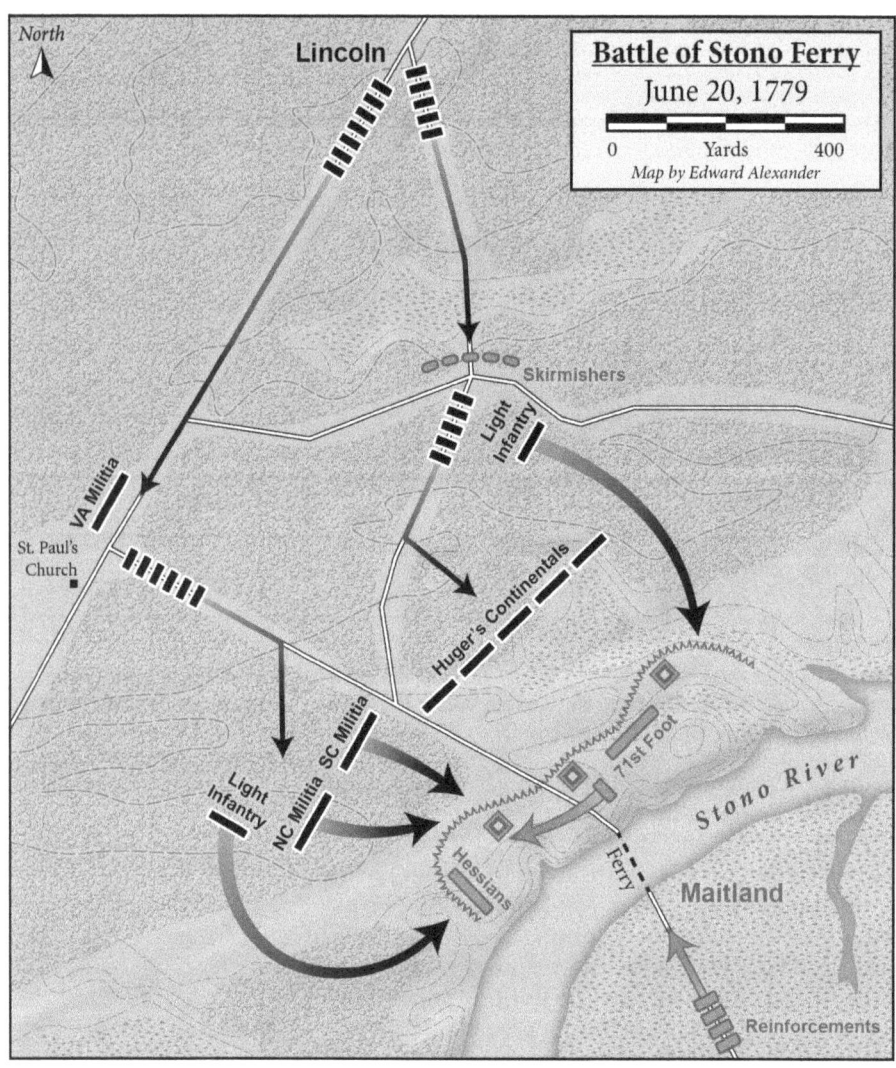

Battle of Stono Ferry—Halting to trade fire with the British regulars, the Continental troops suffered numerous casualties and were unable to dislodge the British from their entrenchments at Stono Ferry. The battle was a painful lesson to the Americans of the need to press attacks with the bayonet. Though a defeat, the Patriots, both Continental and militia, displayed courage and tenacity that bolstered their confidence.

of the attack by the militia, broke and fell back. It appeared for a moment that the British lines would be flanked, but Maitland quickly shifted some of the 71st Regiment from the right flank to shore up the left. The move saved the British army. The Hessians rallied and the firing along the lines continued. The original battle plan was for the South Carolina Continentals under the command of Gen. Isaac Huger to not exchange fire with the British, but to break their lines with a swift bayonet charge. However, because of a creek that passed in front of the British lines and the natural inclination to shoot back while being fired upon, the South Carolinians found themselves in a firefight that they were losing. With the British entrenched and the Continentals in the open field, it was an uneven fight, and American casualties piled up. Lincoln realized that his men needed to assault the British works with their bayonets. He rode in front of Gen. Isaac Huger's Continentals and implored them to stop firing and to charge. The Continentals did not budge, rather they resumed firing. American artillery attempted to batter the British earthworks but had little effect. Colonel Owen Roberts, the commander of the 4th South Carolina Artillery, was mortally wounded during the intense fighting.

General Isaac Huger led Continental troops at the battle of Stono Ferry. (nypl)

After an hour, British reinforcements arrived on the mainland side of the river. Realizing that the battle was lost, Lincoln ordered a retreat and the Americans fell back in an orderly fashion. The British looked to harass the retreating Americans and left their entrenchments to attack their rear, but the Americans unleashed a heavy fire on them and convinced the British to fall back to the ferry.

The Americans were beaten back, but they had fought well and bravely. The British suffered heavy casualties: 26 killed and 103 wounded. The Americans also suffered, having 34 killed and 112 wounded. General Isaac Huger was wounded and Colonel Roberts died. Among the American dead was 16-year-old Private Hugh Jackson of the South Carolina militia. His younger brother, 12-year-old Andrew, was serving as a messenger during the battle and was wounded as well. The younger Jackson later became a celebrated general in the War of 1812 and the seventh President of the United States.

In the following days, the British continued their retreat to Georgia, moving first to Beaufort and ultimately to Savannah. Lincoln's army remained south of Charleston waiting to see what the British attempted next.

That summer, news arrived in Charleston that a French fleet under the command of Comte d'Estaing was coming north from the West Indies, its target the British stronghold of Savannah. His fleet arrived outside of the city in September, but because d'Estaing's troops and ships needed supplies,

Comte d'Estaing worked with Gen. Benjamin Lincoln to lay siege to the British occupied city of Savannah. (nypl)

THE BRAVE BOY OF THE WAXHAWS.

Andrew Jackson, the Seventh President of the United States, in 1780 when a boy of 13 enlisted in the cause of his country and was taken prisoner by the British. Being ordered by an officer to clean his boots, he indignantly refused and received a sword cut for his temerity.

Though Andrew Jackson is more famous for his service in the War of 1812, he grew up in South Carolina during the Revolutionary War. His brother died at Stono Ferry and he served as a courier during the battle. Later, he was imprisoned by the British at Camden, South Carolina, and in this depiction, refused to shine a British officer's boots and was struck by the officer. (loc)

they spent the better part of the next month making repairs and preparing to attack the city. The delay allowed the British to recall their men into Savannah and strengthen the city's defenses.

In mid-September, Lincoln and his army of about 3,000 men arrived outside of Savannah. In an attempt to work with their new French allies, Lincoln planned a joint assault on the British position. What followed was a disaster for the American and French forces.

By the end of September, the French began constructing earthworks to lay siege to the city of Savannah. The two sides bombarded each other with artillery through early October, but it was becoming clear that an assault would have to be attempted to end the siege.

In the foggy early morning hours of October 9, 1779, d'Estaing and Lincoln launched a combined frontal assault on the Spring Hill Redoubt in Savannah. But it was poorly executed, and instead of a large, coordinated assault, the men charged in piecemeal fashion, which turned the battle into a bloody meat grinder. D'Estaing personally led the French vanguard across the 400 yards of open fields in front of the redoubt. After hacking their way through an abatis, the Frenchmen covered the last 50 yards but sank into a ditch in front of the large earthwork. They then had to scale their way up to the top of the earthen ramparts. So dire was this advance that the men were ordered to not return fire under the threat of death (Lincoln attempted to prevent a repeat of the disaster at Stono Ferry where his men stopped to return fire). The initial French attack was pushed back, but on came another. D'Estaing was wounded in the arm and leg as he rallied his wavering men. A third French column then launched into the redoubt, and it too was pushed back. Wave after wave of French troops assaulted the lightly defended redoubt only to have concentrated musket and cannon fire trained on them each time. Bodies piled up in the ditch and in front of the redoubt.

Then the Americans took the field. General Casimir Pulaski and his cavalry gallantly charged on horseback towards the redoubt, but as they closed on the enemy line a British cannon fired grapeshot and Pulaski was hit and fell mortally wounded from his horse. Lieutenant Colonel John Laurens led the first American infantry column across the bloody ground towards the Spring Hill Redoubt. With him were Virginia levies and the venerable 2nd South Carolina Regiment under the command of Lt. Col. Francis Marion, with many of the heroes from the battle of Sullivan's Island. Flying above their weapons were

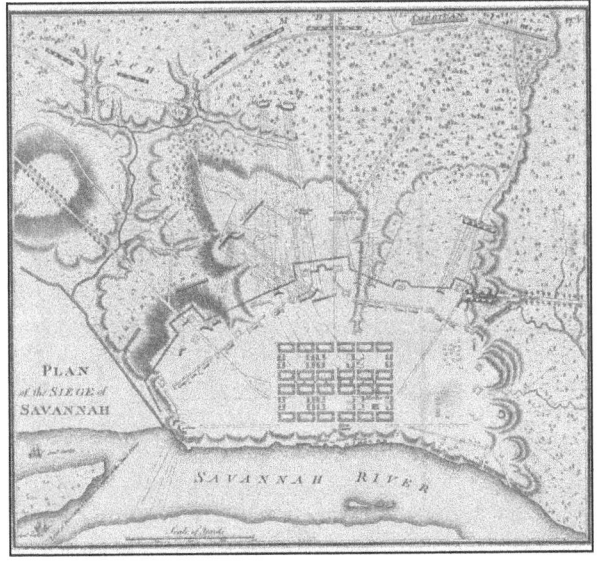

A map from period of the siege of Savannah in 1779.
(nypl)

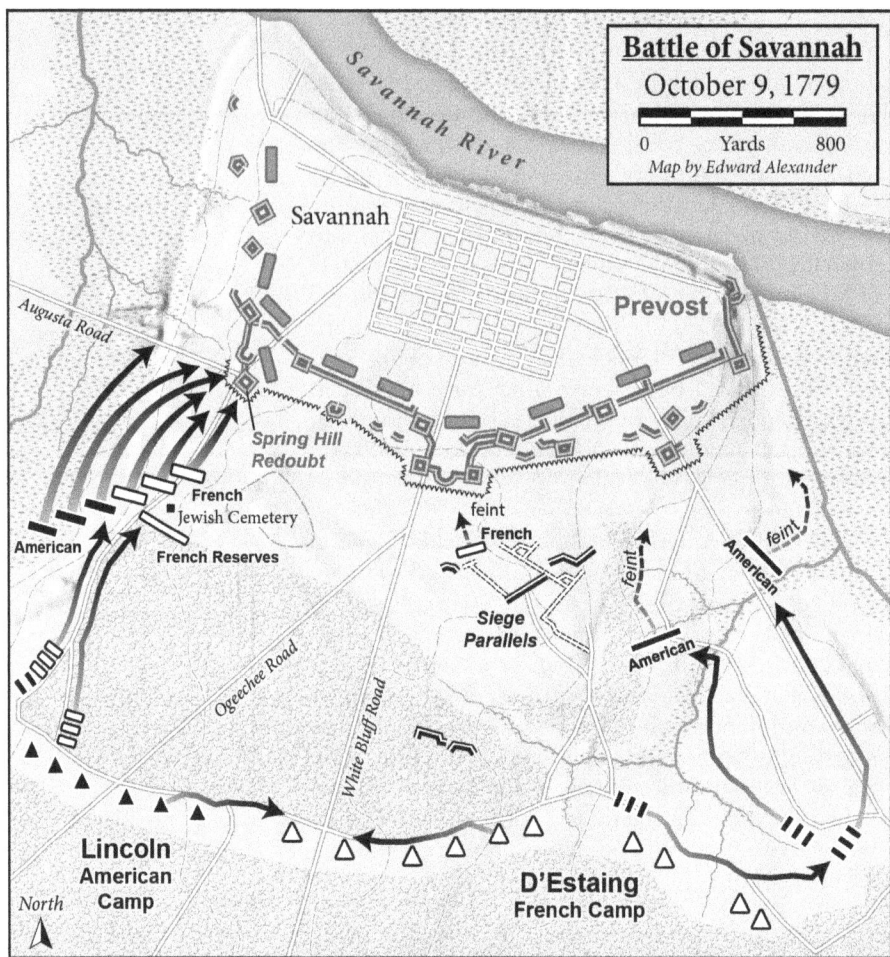

BATTLE OF SAVANNAH—The American and French assaults on the morning of October 9, 1779 were some of the bloodiest assaults of the Revolutionary War. Nearly 800 men were killed or wounded in the piecemeal assaults on the British Spring Hill Redoubt.

two regimental flags that had been presented to them following that earlier victory. Lieutenants John Bush and Alexander Hume bore these flags and bravely forced their way to the top of the redoubt and planted them on the rampart. The victory was momentary, though. A volley of musketry cut both men down. Lieutenant James Gray grabbed one of the flags and the venerable Sgt. William Jasper grabbed the other. Sergeant Jasper, vaunted for his heroics saving the flag at the battle of Sullivan's Island, now held his regiment's colors on the Spring Hill Redoubt in the center of the violent storm of battle. Neither Gray nor Jasper lasted long. Shortly after grabbing the

In this drawing, Casmir Pulaski falls from his horse mortally wounded. (nypl)

flags, they too were killed by the British fire. Four men died attempting to plant the colors of the 2nd South Carolina at Savannah. The men endured vicious fighting for nearly an hour, after which the attacks were called off and the men retreated from the field. One of the flags was captured by the British, while the other was brought back with Sgt. Jasper who

William Jasper plants the flag of the 2nd South Carolina on the rampart of the Spring Hill Redoubt before being shot down. (nypl)

Memorial stones are laid out on the ground where hundreds of French and American troops died while assaulting the Spring Hill Redoubt. (psg)

was carried back by the Americans off the battlefield. Jasper, with one of his last gasps of breath, told a fellow soldier, "Tell Mrs. Elliott I lost my life supporting the colors she presented to our regiment."

With the field littered with the dead and dying, the battle resulted in an utter defeat for the French and Americans. They had attacked with nearly 4,000 men, and nearly 1,000 were killed, wounded, or captured. Among the dead were bona fide heroes, including Casimir Pulaski and William Jasper. The British, on the other hand, had lost fewer than 100 casualties.

D'Estaing immediately lifted the siege and prepared to return to the West Indies; Lincoln and his army prepared to retreat to Charleston in defeat. The poor communication and planning between Lincoln and d'Estaing were major factors contributing to the ultimate defeat at Savannah. Lincoln did his best to keep his Southern army together, but many of his best troops perished in front of the Spring Hill Redoubt

and the militia began deserting in large numbers. Returning to France to recover from his wounds, d'Estaing would not see combat again. He lived until 1794, when he was ultimately caught up in the French Reign of Terror and executed by guillotine.

When Henry Clinton in New York learned of the British victory at Savannah, he was ecstatic. He exclaimed that "I think this is the greatest event

A statue in Madison Square in Savannah, Georgia, depicts Sgt. William Jasper being shot down holding the flag of the 2nd South Carolina Regiment. (mm)

that has happened [in] the whole war." Clinton immediately started preparations for sending more troops and ships to the south. All of a sudden, the British high command was injected with a wave of optimism for the plan to subdue the South.

Clinton quickly turned his attention to the South Carolina city that had thus far escaped capture: Charleston.

A recreation of the Spring Hill Redoubt sits on the location where the original redoubt once stood. (psg)

Driving Tour 2

This tour begins at the site of the battle of Stono Ferry (June 20, 1779) and goes across James Island, West Ashley, Summerville, North Charleston, and ends at downtown Charleston. On this tour you will see sites associated with the 1779 attack on Charleston, the British advance on the city in 1780, and the site of the final skirmish that happened in South Carolina in 1782.

GPS: N 32.748583, W 80.164423

Tour Stop 1 – Stono Ferry Battlefield

After Prevost left Charleston, he maintained a rear guard here at Stono Ferry that was attacked by General Lincoln's army on June 19, 1779. The American army engaged in a violent firefight with entrenched British soldiers, their backs to the Stono River. Almost 300 men were killed or wounded

in this battle. Today, much of the battlefield is occupied by a golf course, The Links at Stono Ferry, however, you can access the area where the British left flank was anchored. That area is part of Old Wide Awake Park. There is no interpretation about the battle currently in the park, but it offers a great view of where the ferry once was on the Stono River.

Today, much of the battlefield where the battle of Stono Ferry occurred is under the Links at Stono Ferry golf course. However, the area where the British left flank was can be seen at Old Wide Awake Park. From here, you can see where the ferry once was on the Stono River. (mm)

5035 Trexler Ave., Hollywood, SC 29449
GPS: N 32.748583, W 80.164423

➡ TO TOUR STOP 2

Turn right out of Trexler Ave., onto SC-162. Go 2 miles and then make a slight right onto US-17 N. Stay on US-17 N for 1.4 miles crossing over Rantowles Creek. Make a U-turn at Towles Crossing Dr. and cross back over Rantowles Creek. After crossing the creek, make your first right onto State Rd. S-10-1840. Follow the road for 0.5 miles to a dead end. Park on the street and follow a dirt path that leads to a brick enclosed cemetery.

GPS: N 32.799667, W 80.141750

Tour Stop 2 — William Washington's Grave

William Washington, a distant cousin of George Washington, played an important role in the Revolutionary War. Originally from Stafford County, Virginia, Washington joined the Continental army as an officer in the 3rd Virginia regiment and was wounded at the battle of Trenton. He then joined the

A twentieth century tombstone marks the final resting place of William Washington and his wife. The backside of the tombstone incorrectly claims he fought at Lexington and Bunker Hill. (mm)

Continental Light Dragoons and in 1780 was sent to fight in South Carolina. Washington fought in most of the significant actions of the Southern theater. In 1782, Washington married Jane Elliot and moved to the Elliot plantation at Sandy Hill near Rantowles' Bridge (the same location where Washington fought in a skirmish with Banastre Tarleton in 1780). Washington died in 1810 and was buried here on the Sandy Hill estate. His gravestone says he was at Lexington and Concord and Bunker Hill even though he was not. A much more elaborate gravestone was created in the mid-19th century to mark his grave, but instead was placed in Magnolia Cemetery where it stands today as a cenotaph.

Ravenel, SC 29470
GPS: N 32.799667, W 80.141750

TO TOUR STOP 3

Drive back out on State Rd. S-10-1840 to US-17. Turn right onto US-17 S. In 0.3 miles make a U-Turn and drive on US-17 N for 10 miles. Turn right onto Wesley Dr., which turns into State Hwy 171/Folly Rd. Stay on this for 1.5 miles then turn left onto Harbor View Rd. Stay on this for 1.7 miles and immediately after crossing over James Island Creek, turn right onto N Shore Dr. Stay on N Shore Dr. for 0.4 miles and you will see the historic marker on your right.

GPS: N 32.744463, W 79.947498

Tour Stop 3 - Dills Bluff Battlefield

James Island, South Carolina, has the distinction of not only being the site of the first shot of the American Civil War, but also the last shot of the Revolutionary War. It was here at Dills Bluff where the last blood was spilled in America during the Revolution. Here, a contingent of Americans attacked a small group of British soldiers, and Captain William Wilmot became the last death of the Revolution on November 14, 1782. Today a state historic marker denotes the location of this final action.

701 Dills Bluff Court, Charleston, SC 29412
GPS: N 32.744463, W 79.947498

The British Advance on Charleston

CHAPTER FIVE

FEBRUARY–MARCH 1780

*"The Enemys present disposition of his force and all
his late operations indicate a design to attack
Charles Town by a siege in form."*

— Lt. Col. John Laurens to
Gen. George Washington, March 14, 1780

General Sir Henry Clinton was unhappy with the situation in New York City. He and his army of 19,000 men sat staring at Washington and his army of 12,000 men in New York and New Jersey. The British had lost minor battles at Stony Point and Paulus Hook, but overall, the two armies were locked in a stalemate. Clinton was eager to make some movements in the southern states, and both he and George Germain in London saw great potential in South Carolina. Especially encouraged after Prevost's small army had been able to march to and threaten Charleston, they believed with a large enough army they could subdue the entire region. Clinton, though, was wary of going to sea while d'Estaing's naval force was off the coast of Georgia. However, upon hearing of the disaster at Savannah and that d'Estaing was leaving the seas open, the opportunity arose for Clinton to move south.

Leaving 10,000 troops in New York City, on December 26, 1779, Henry Clinton sailed for Georgia with nearly 9,000 Crown forces and 30 warships. They arrived in Savannah near the end of January 1780. Numerous storms made the five-week journey a harrowing affair, but the focus of the war just made a dramatic shift to the south.

Upon arriving in Georgia waters, Clinton's force regrouped and resupplied before going on the attack. On February 11, 1780, Clinton and his large force sailed out of Savannah toward Charleston, but this time he would avoid the fort on Sullivan's Island that

The view of downtown Charleston from Fort Johnson. From here the British got their first view of the city during their approach in February of 1780. (mm)

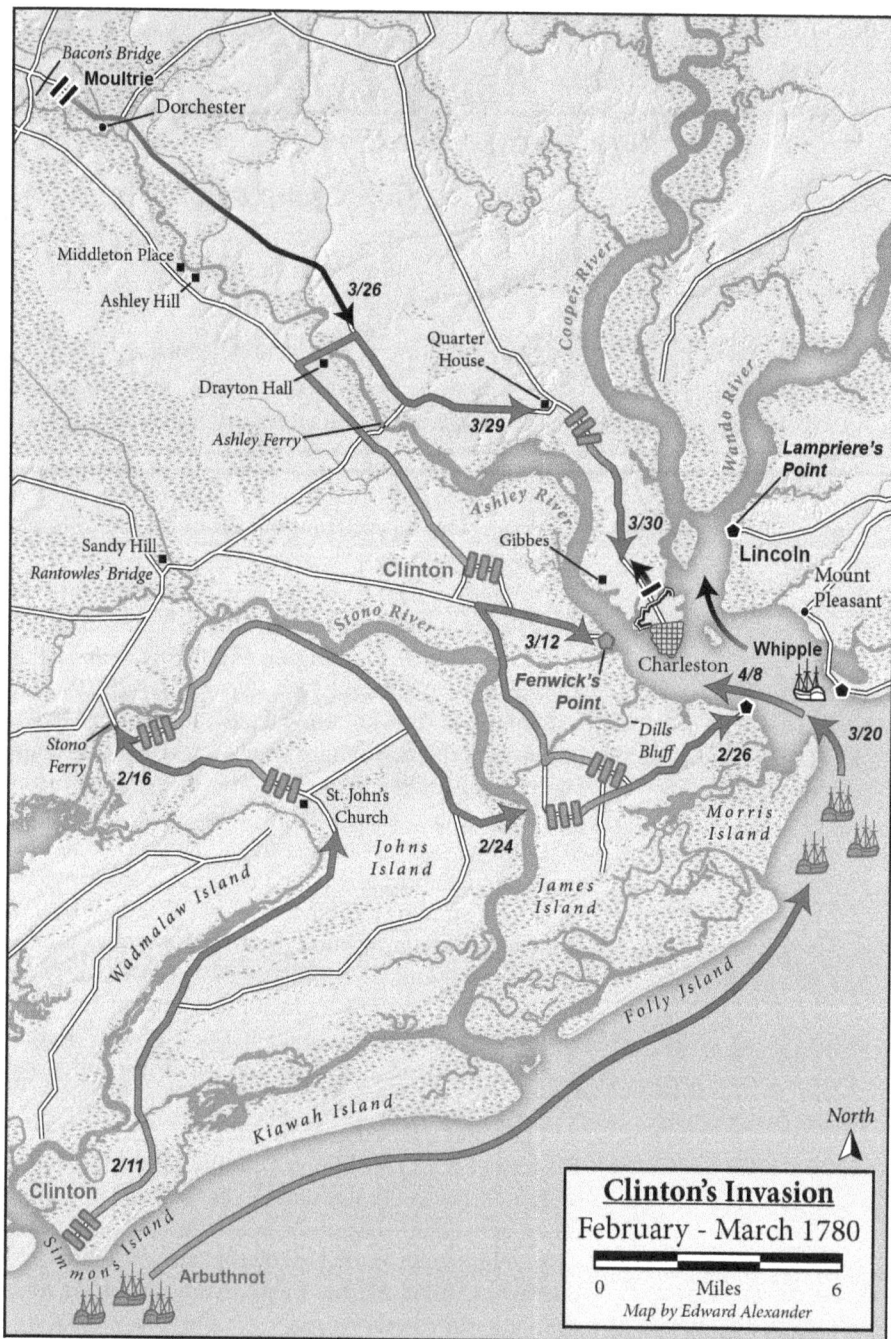

CLINTON'S INVASION—With no way to stop their advance, in 1780 the British methodically and relentlessly moved overland across the sea islands south of Charleston to cut the city off and force its submission.

ruined their plans in 1776. Instead, he landed his army 25 miles southwest of Charleston on the southern tip of Simmons Island (modern-day Seabrook Island). The British would march overland following a similar path that Prevost had used the year before and try to cut off the city on the peninsula by land. The British began the march with more than three times the number of men and ships as the previous invasions in 1776 and 1779. This would be the most determined effort to capture Charleston in the war.

The city erupted into a panic and many Charlestonians fled. However, Prevost's army had shown them the previous year that if they fled, their homes and property would be susceptible to looting and destruction. Before ending their current session, the state legislature gave Governor John Rutledge expanded executive power. Rutledge called up the militia to defend the town, but many refused to go due to a recent smallpox outbreak in the city. In the end, only a few hundred South Carolina militia joined the main army in this time of extreme peril.

Abraham Whipple commanded the meager Patriot naval forces at the Siege of Charleston in 1780. (nypl)

Learning of the movements of Clinton's army, Washington began directing efforts to help defend Charleston. He repeatedly received letters requesting troops and supplies, but was unaware of how truly desperate the situation was until his former aide-de-camp, Lt. Col. John Laurens, informed him in person. Following his gallant service at the battle of Savannah, Laurens traveled to New York in December and described for Washington the alarming situation in South Carolina. That November Washington had dispatched the North Carolina Continental line regiments (almost 1,000 men), but after talking to Laurens, the commander in chief made the bold decision to send the entire Virginia Continental line regiments (almost 2,500 men) to join Lincoln's army. Among those sent to Charleston was Washington's distant cousin, Col. William Washington, and his cavalry. General Washington parted with these veterans even though it weakened his position guarding against the main British army at New York City. Unable to use the seas due to British Navy, these intrepid North Carolina and Virginia Continentals marched overland from New Jersey to Charleston, a journey of more than 800 miles. During the more than four month long march they also passed through their home states, which proved to be an awful temptation for desertion.

Mariot Arbuthnot commanded the Royal navy during the Siege of Charleston in 1780. (nypl)

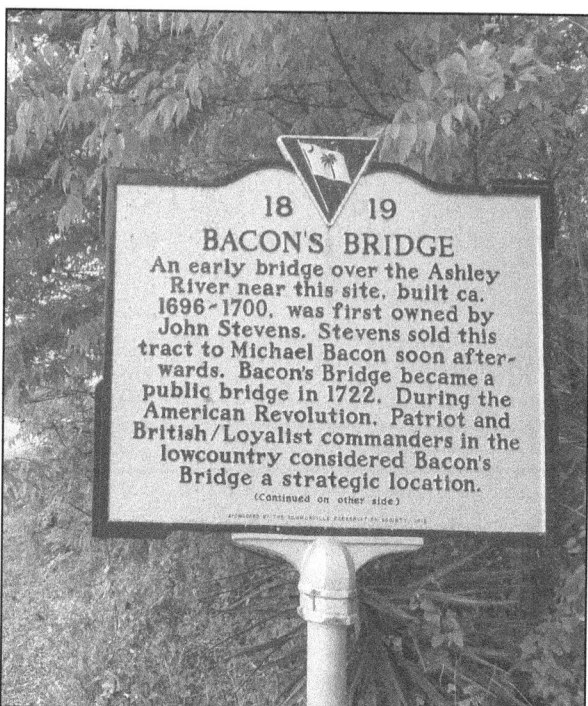

18 19
BACON'S BRIDGE
An early bridge over the Ashley River near this site, built ca. 1696-1700, was first owned by John Stevens. Stevens sold this tract to Michael Bacon soon afterwards. Bacon's Bridge became a public bridge in 1722. During the American Revolution, Patriot and British/Loyalist commanders in the lowcountry considered Bacon's Bridge a strategic location.
(Continued on other side)

Bacon's Bridge was a strategic crossing on the Ashley River. (mm)

While Lincoln patiently waited for these desperately needed reinforcements, he began to look to the defense of the city. He was in a dire position. Lincoln wanted to attack Clinton on the march but was unable to do so due to his lack of manpower. By February 1780, he had fewer than 2,400 Continentals and militia to defend the town from the British force, which was almost three times his army's size. With these staggering odds, Lincoln made the decision to stay in Charleston and fight. He was criticized for this decision, but at the time it made sense. In 1779, Lincoln had made the mistake of leaving Charleston, and the city nearly fell. He was under pressure from both the Continental Congress and state and local leaders to make a defense, and, like Washington during the New York and Philadelphia campaigns, decided to defer to civilian authority. There was no way his small army could attack the much larger British force in the open, so he decided a defensive strategy would even the odds. He had also received word that the reinforcements from the north were on their way and that he may just need to hold out until they arrived. All these factors convinced Lincoln to stay and defend Charleston.

Slaves and soldiers worked feverishly to reinforce the defenses constructed the previous year and to build new ones. Lincoln, unsure how Clinton would approach the city, bolstered the defenses at Fort Moultrie (in addition to those on the Charleston Neck) to be prepared for another possible attack by sea. Since the victory on Sullivan's Island in 1776, Fort Moultrie had been completed and was guarded by 200 men and 40 cannon. They hoped the fort could withstand another attack from the Royal navy. Due to manpower shortages, Lincoln decided to abandon Fort Johnson on the southern side of the harbor.

A small American naval force under the command of Commander Abraham Whipple arrived to help defend the city. Whipple had six frigates, a sloop of war, and numerous smaller vessels. Lincoln was confident the naval forces would stand well along with the forts against a British attempt to take the harbor.

The main line of defense on the neck was an earthen trench that stretched between the Ashley and Cooper Rivers, near the city gate. In front of it was a dug canal that formed a type of moat to further protect the defenders. Just behind the center of this main defensive line was a large redoubt made of tabby called the Hornwork. This massive, enclosed fortification was originally constructed during the French and Indian War and served as the central location of the American defenses. The Hornwork was more than 700 feet long and its tabby walls were described by a French observer as being about 30 feet tall. If the British attempted a frontal assault against the city, they would have to cross the dug canal, work through two lines of abatis, scale the earthen parapet of the American position, and then enter the tabby Hornwork, all while under a constant fire.

Sir Henry Clinton remembered the failed attack he took part in on June 28, 1776, and did not want to make the same mistakes. To capture Charleston, he planned a two-pronged attack: the army would move up along the islands to the south and west of Charleston and cut off the peninsula while Adm. Mariot Arbuthnot with the Royal navy, instead of engaging in a cannon duel with the forts, would quickly sail past the Patriot forts and into the harbor. The largest hindrance to this plan would be the teamwork between Clinton's and Arbuthnot's forces. Clinton did not work well with Cmdr. Peter Parker in 1776, and the result was a disaster. Clinton also did not

Hessian Captain Johann Ewald's diary has great details about the 1780 siege of Charleston. After the Revolutionary War, Ewald went on to become a general in the Danish army. (wiki)

get along well with Arbuthnot, which could portend another disaster.

After the unopposed landing on February 11, the British began their march across the islands toward the city of Charleston. The march was difficult as the terrain was filled with swamps, marshes, and creeks. The European troops having just arrived from New York were likely surprised to see this type of environment, including the insects and probably animals such as alligators. One Hessian exclaimed: "What a land to wage war in!" The British soon worked their way up to Johns Island. Lincoln dispatched the Patriot cavalry to attack and harass the British columns as they moved up Johns Island, but they were unable to do much damage or slow their march.

On February 16, Clinton reached the Stono River. As the British marched through the islands, just as Prevost's army had the previous year, they destroyed, plundered, stole, and raped the South Carolina countryside. Many of the civilians became targets, and soldiers mistreated the elderly, women, and children they encountered. Anyone who may have been on the fence in this conflict was quickly compelled to join the Patriot side. Major John Andre, a British officer, hated this. Henry Clinton disapproved as well but did nothing to stop it. One British soldier noticed on the faces of many of the Lowcountry residents that "they hated us from the bottom of their hearts."

On February 24, Clinton crossed the Stono River and landed on James Island and immediately occupied the abandoned Fort Johnson, giving the British their first view of the church steeples of Charleston. A few days later, Commodore Whipple dispatched a ship in the harbor to begin firing on the British troops at Fort Johnson, which forced them to seek cover. However, Lincoln was essentially powerless at this point to stop the British from continuing their march towards the vulnerable city.

Lincoln received much needed reinforcements when the North Carolina Continental brigade under the command of Gen. James Hogun arrived on March 3 after their 800-mile trek. This reinforcement gave "great spirit to the town, and confidence to the Army" and added 760 muskets to his ranks. Lincoln now commanded approximately 4,300 men. Most of these were stationed in the city, but some were at Fort Moultrie and others were up at Bacon's Bridge (modern-day Summerville) to prevent the British from crossing the Ashley River near there.

Like an unstoppable force, on March 10 Clinton crossed the Wappoo Creek onto the mainland of modern-day West Ashley. Clinton built a battery on Fenwick's Point (modern-day Albemarle Point) directly across the Ashley River from Charleston, and by March 12 the city of Charleston, a mile away, was within the range of British cannon. More importantly, the British cannon there prevented American ships from navigating the Ashley River. At this point, Clinton wanted to wait for Arbuthnot to enter the harbor to help ferry troops across the Ashley River and to keep from extending his own forces too far from their supply base.

William Woodford of Caroline County, Virginia, was a real hero of the Revolutionary War. Having distinguished himself in combat at the battles of Great Bridge and Brandywine, he led the Virginia brigade on its march to Charleston in the spring of 1780. Captured in the Siege of Charleston, he grew ill in captivity and was sent to New York City in an attempt to aid him, but he died of illness while imprisoned by the British. (chs)

Lincoln, still waiting in Charleston, was working to get the siege lines in the city up to strength. Despite improvements to the defense lines, the manpower issue made the situation much more difficult for Lincoln. On March 24, some of the North Carolina militia simply up and left after their term expired.

On March 20, Arbuthnot and his British ships sailed over the Charleston Bar. Whipple, surprised the Royal navy was able to move all their ships over the bar, now realized his small flotilla could not stop them from entering the harbor. Whipple had planned to stop the British by having his ships sit next to Fort Moultrie, but realizing this was not possible, left the harbor and sailed his flotilla into the Cooper River just east of the city. The Royal navy now had to contend solely with Fort Moultrie. The Patriots hoped the defenders of Fort Moultrie would repeat their improbable victory of 1776 and repel Arbuthnot's vessels.

On March 26, Gen. William Moultrie and his outpost at Bacon's Bridge were recalled into the city. With the Royal navy just outside the harbor and the British army just across the Ashley River, Lincoln was prepared to make a final defense of the city. The battle for Charleston in 1780 would come down to classic 18th-century siege warfare.

Clinton needed to cross the Ashley River to then descend on the Americans at Charleston. But rather than travel all the way up to Bacon's Bridge and cross, or cross close to the city where they might be attacked, Clinton chose to cross at Drayton Hall, the home of William Henry Drayton, a Continental congressman who had died in 1779. In the early morning hours of March 29, the British army crossed the Ashley River at Drayton Hall and started towards Charleston. By evening, Clinton's invading force was only six miles from the American defenses and made camp near the Quarter house.

The next morning, two and a half miles from Charleston, the British vanguard met their first resistance. A party of American riflemen opened fire on them, and then kept up a fighting retreat to a small redoubt or fleche about a mile in front of the city defenses. These riflemen were under the command of Lt. Col. John Laurens. Laurens had about 200 men (both riflemen and light infantry) posted in front of the main defenses. Laurens wanted Lincoln to send him artillery to keep up the fight, but Lincoln wanted Laurens to fall back to the main defenses. The British light infantry and Hessian jaegers drove Laurens and his men from their redoubt, but as they were falling back to town, reinforcements and artillery arrived. Laurens made the bold decision to charge the British and take back the redoubt.

The Hessians and Patriots engaged in brutal hand-to-hand combat. Hessian Capt. Johann Ewald noted that the Americans attacked with "considerable violence." Though Laurens and his men temporarily held the redoubt, British light infantry reinforcements overwhelmed them, and the Patriots were forced back to the city's main defenses. Clinton halted his troops so they would not be lured into a trap. The fighting was limited and both sides suffered only a few casualties, each side suffering approximately 30 men killed and wounded. Laurens and his men had ceded the ground to the British and Hessian forces but were invigorated by their ability to fight the redcoats in the open. The Hessians and British were also pleased with their performance and waited for the rest of the army to join them on the Charleston Neck as the siege of Charleston began.

 **TO TOUR STOP 4**

Turn around and drive back up N Shore Dr. for 0.2 miles. Turn right onto Waites Dr. In 0.2 miles turn right onto Harbor View Dr. Stay on Harbor View Dr. for 1.8 miles and take the 3rd exit in the roundabout onto Fort Johnson Rd. Follow this road for 1.2 miles entering the marine research facility. There is a parking lot near the cisterns and powder magazine.

GPS: N 32.751500, W 79.897974

Tour Stop 4 — Fort Johnson

This is the location of Fort Johnson. Today, the area is a marine research station. You can still see two colonial-era cisterns made of tabby and a colonial brick powder magazine with a plaque to Colonel Moultrie raising the first flag of American liberty on the site. Fort Johnson was not engaged in 1776. In 1779, the fort was destroyed by the Patriots so the British would be unable to use it. In 1780, Patriots further destroyed the remnants before Henry Clinton and his men captured the area. Today the site offers great panoramic views of Charleston and the entire harbor. Perhaps more important in the site's history was the fact that the first shot of the American Civil War was fired from this position at Fort Sumter on the morning of April 12, 1861. There is a commemorative marker on the site today.

Fort Johnson Rd., Charleston, SC 29412
GPS: N 32.751500, W 79.897974

⟹ TO TOUR STOP 5

Head south on Fort Johnson Rd. for 1.2 miles. At the traffic circle, take the second exit onto Harbor View Rd. Stay on Harbor View Rd. for 3 miles. Turn right to merge onto SC-30 E toward Downtown. Stay on SC-30 for 0.7 miles and take exit 1 toward SC-61/Summerville. Stay on SC-61 for 11 miles. Turn right into Drayton Hall.

GPS: N 32.870961, W 80.076273

Tour Stop 5 — Drayton Hall

Drayton Hall was the home of William Henry Drayton, who was a delegate to the Continental Congress in Philadelphia when he died of disease in 1779. This was the location where the British crossed the Ashley River in March 1780. Today this historic site is open to the public and its history is interpreted by the Drayton Hall Preservation Trust.

3380 Ashley River Rd., Charleston, SC 29414
(N 32.870961, W 80.076273)

The British crossed the Ashley River near Drayton Hall and Magnolia Plantation. Clinton used Drayton Hall as his headquarters during this time. (loc)

 **TO TOUR STOP 6**

Head north on SC-61 for 4.3 miles and turn right into Middleton Place.

GPS: N 32.900144, W 80.136445

Tour Stop 6 – Middleton Place

At Middleton Place is the tomb of Arthur Middleton, one of the signers of the Declaration of Independence. Buried in the same tomb is his grandson, Williams Middleton, a signer of South Carolina's Ordinance of Secession. (mm)

Middleton Place was the plantation home of signer of the Declaration of Independence Arthur Middleton. The home was burned by Union soldiers during the Civil War, and the ruins collapsed as a result of the 1886 earthquake. Despite this, the grounds, gardens, and rebuilt wing of the house interpret the site's colonial and Revolutionary War history. The adjacent Inn at Middleton Place is situated on the site of Ashley Hill plantation. This was where Greene's Continental army encamped while awaiting the evacuation of the British soldiers from Charleston. More than 200 men died of disease at the hospital here and today they likely lie in unmarked graves.

4300 Ashley River Rd., Charleston, SC 29414
GPS: N 32.900144, W 80.136445

TO TOUR STOP 7

Head north on SC-61 for 4.9 miles. Turn right onto Bacon's Bridge Rd. (SC-165) In 0.3 miles make a slight right to stay on Bacon's Bridge Rd. Drive for 1.2 miles, traveling over the Ashley River at the historic site of Bacon's Bridge. Turn right onto Dorchester Rd. (SC-642) and drive for 2 miles. Turn right onto County Rd. S-18-373. Follow this road to the parking lot in 0.3 miles.

GPS: N 32.948989, W 80.169817

Tour Stop 7 – Colonial Dorchester State Historic Site

Colonial Dorchester is a state park that interprets the fort and town that once stood here. You can see an original tabby fort that dates to the French and Indian War. It was also here that Moultrie crossed the Ashley River as he was falling back towards Charleston in May of 1779. The site is open to the public and is well interpreted by the South Carolina State Park Service.

TO TOUR STOP 8

Head back out to Dorchester Rd. and turn right. Stay on Dorchester Rd. for 14.5 miles and the intersection with Rivers Ave. This intersection is the approximate location of the historic Quarter house.

GPS: N 32.856707, W 79.979060

(ABOVE) Just as in 1779, in 1780 the British burned and looted as they tramped across the area. One victim was the St. George Church in Colonial Dorchester which still stands as a haunting reminder of the cost of war. (mm)

The tabby walls of Fort Dorchester are a good example of the material that was used to construct the Hornwork in Charleston. (mm)

Colonial Fort Dorchester still stands near Summerville, South Carolina. This French and Indian War fort became actively used during the Revolutionary War. (mm)

Tour Stop 8 – The Quarter House

This was the general area near where the Quarter House was located and where the British camped on their way to Charleston. (mm)

This is approximately the location of the Quarter house encampment. The British vanguard camped near here on the evening of March 29, 1780, just six miles from the city. Today, there is nothing marking the site.

3503 Rivers Ave., North Charleston, SC 29405
GPS: N 32.856707, W 79.979060

 **TO TOUR STOP 9**

Head south on River Ave. toward Downtown. In 3.4 miles, Rivers Ave. turns into King St. Continue another 1.2 miles then turn right onto Moultrie St. Follow Moultrie St. as it turns into Lee Ave. on the Citadel campus and turn right onto Hammond Ave.

GPS: N 32.796107, W 79.962388

Tour Stop 9 — Gibbes Plantation

This is where some of the Hessians camped before opening the siege of Charleston. The John Gibbes plantation became a major depot for the British army as they ferried troops, equipment, and artillery across the Ashley River. Much of the British materiel for war was located here as they engaged in the 42-day siege of the city. Today, the site is the location of the Citadel, a military college.

The view from the site of Gibbes's plantation on the Citadel campus today looking towards the west and the Ashley River. (mm)

2 Hammond Ave., Charleston, SC 29403
GPS: N 32.796107, W 79.962388

TO TOUR STOP 10

Turn left onto Lee Ave. and head back off the Citadel's campus. Stay on Lee Ave./Moultrie St. for 0.6 miles and turn right onto King St. Go one block to the intersection of King St. and Huger St.

GPS: N 32.800230, W 79.948383

Tour Stop 10 — Laurens's Fleche

It was in this approximate location that the opening engagement of the siege of Charleston occurred on March 30, 1780. A fleche was a small earthwork that was open in the rear. After opening fire on the British vanguard about two and a half miles from the city, Laurens' men fought a running battle back to this fleche. After fighting here, they were pushed back even farther. Laurens' men then charged back into and temporarily recaptured the fleche before being pushed back to the main American defenses. About 60 men were killed and wounded in all this fighting, some in hand-to-hand combat. This area of King St. has been heavily developed and nothing denotes the importance of this location.

888 King St., Charleston, SC 29403
GPS: N 32.800230, W 79.948383

▶ TO TOUR STOP 11

Continue down King St. for 0.5 miles. Turn left onto Line St. The next intersection is Meeting St. and the site of the New Market Race Course.

GPS: N 32.796166, W 79.940440

This is near the location where Laurens's fleche was located. There was brutal hand-to-hand combat that occurred in this area. (mm)

Tour Stop 11 – Pulaski Legion Battle Site

This is where the New Market Race Course (a colonial horse race track) was located. In 1779, this was open ground. On May 11, 1779, near here, Gen. Casimir Pulaski's light infantry and cavalry engaged the British in a brief but ferocious fight. Pulaski commanded 60 cavalrymen and 60 light infantry. He ordered his command to charge a position of 40 British dragoons and several hundred British infantry. The British suffered only two killed and four wounded, while Pulaski suffered 14 killed and 42 taken prisoner. Pulaski pulled back to the safety of the main city fortifications. Today this battle site is heavily developed with no interpretation.

492 Meeting St., Charleston, SC 29403
GPS: N 32.796166, W 79.940440

This is the approximate location of the New Market Race Course where Pulaski's Legion fought on May 11, 1779. (mm)

The Siege of Charleston

CHAPTER SIX

APRIL–MAY 1780

"… the mortars from both sides threw out an immense number of shells; it was a glorious sight, to see them like meteors crossing each other, and bursting in the air; it appeared as if the stars were tumbling down."

— Gen. William Moultrie

Clinton was impressed by the American fortifications at Charleston, describing them as "by no means contemptible." Rather than launch a costly frontal assault on the American position, which could result in a disaster such as Savannah had been for the Americans, he would build fortifications, lay siege to the town, and force the garrison to surrender.

The area around John Gibbes's plantation, on the Charleston Neck less than a mile and a half from the main American defensive line, became the major supply location for the British siege effort. A ferry was set up to shuttle all the material for war across the Ashley River from Lining's Creek. On April 1, Clinton dispatched his engineer, Maj. James Moncrief, to begin building trenches and redoubts to protect the approaching British and Hessian troops.

They first built three redoubts on the night of April 1, just 800 yards from the main American defenses. All the ground between the two armies was open. As the British approached the city, General Lincoln ordered all the trees and buildings in this area to be cut down or destroyed, making those 800 yards a desolate no man's land. When the Americans awoke on April 2 to see these British works, they immediately opened fire upon them with artillery. However, the American artillery fire did little damage.

These redoubts would eventually be connected by earthen trenches. This line of trenches and redoubts was referred to as a "parallel" since they ran parallel to

This 19th century print by Alonzo Chappel depicts the British constructing parallels on the Charleston neck in 1780. Note the boom depicted from downtown to Shute's Folly. (nypl)

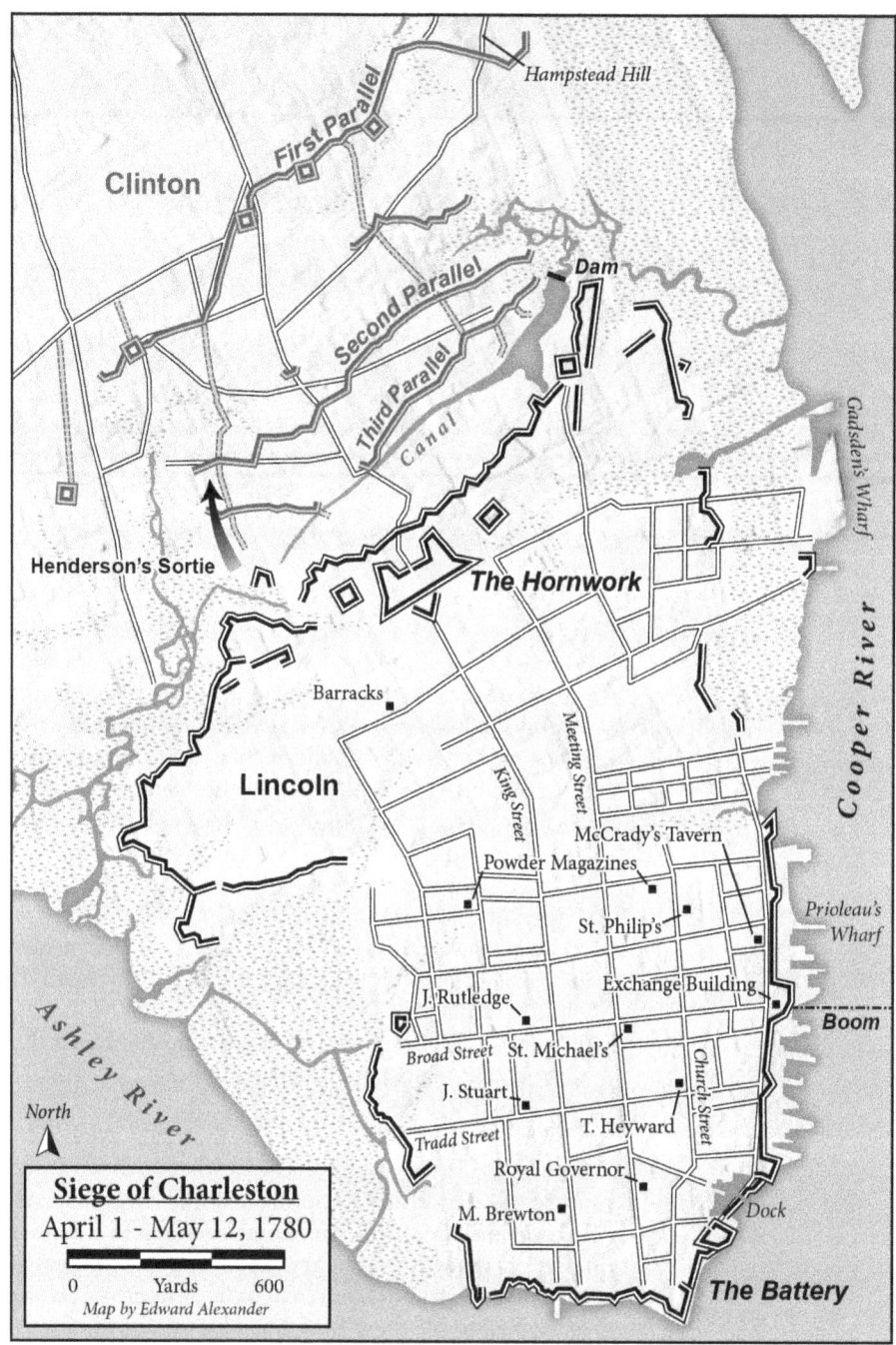

SIEGE OF CHARLESTON—The British employed a formal siege on the city of Charleston that lasted for 42 days.

the defenders' lines. Clinton was planning to construct a parallel, then dig approach trenches toward the city and build another parallel. This way, the army could slowly, safely, and surely bring its artillery eventually to point-blank range and pound the garrison into submission. As the British soldiers and workmen continued to labor furiously on more redoubts and trenches for the first parallel, they were harassed by a constant fire from the American defenders. Because they needed to complete the fortifications in order to bring up their artillery, for the first few days they were unable to return fire on the Americans. As the British worked on the parallel next to the Cooper River, an American ship fired on it as well, before British artillery came up and drove it off.

As work continued under fire, the British employed a brutal tactic. On the night of April 5, Clinton ordered the British artillery at Fenwick's Point and the ships at Wappoo Creek to open fire on the city. But these artillery shells were directed at the civilian population, not on the American defenses. Hessian Captain Johann Ewald noted that as the British shells struck the city, a "terrible clamor" arose from the populace, and the "loud wailing of female voices . . . moved [him] to tears."

Today, Liberty Square is located at the site of Gadsden's wharf where the hundreds of Virginia Continentals arrived into the city of Charleston. (mm)

The Patriots used the steeple of St. Michael's Church as a lookout during the siege in 1780. (nypl)

On April 7, much to the relief of the defenders, about 750 Virginia Continentals who were dispatched by George Washington finally arrived in Charleston to the cheers of the Americans. The Virginians, under the command of Gen. William Woodford, had marched from New Jersey to Petersburg, Virginia between December and March. On March 8, Woodford began a forced march of his men south. Woodford's men marched almost 18 miles a day to cover the last 505 miles to Charleston in less than 30 days. Outside of Charleston, they boarded boats just north of the city and sailed down the Wando River into the Cooper River, passing the British before landing at Gadsden's Wharf. One Patriot said they "wear the appearance of, what they are in reality, hardy veterans." These battle-tested soldiers under the command of General Woodford marched straight into the American defenses. The Patriot defenders fired their cannons in salute and St. Michael's Church bells pealed all day. Woodford noted that "The Garrison appear in high Spirits, & our arrival seem'd to give them fresh confidence." Among these Continentals were veterans of the battles of New York, Trenton, Princeton, Brandywine, Germantown, and Monmouth. The British were aware, too, that regular soldiers were worth almost twice as much when positioned behind fortifications. Accompanying Woodford's Virginians were almost 200 North Carolina militiamen. With these additions, Lincoln now had about 5,600 men, both Continental and militia, to defend the town.

As Charleston rejoiced, the British were angry that the city's garrison had been reinforced. Clinton seemed unconcerned, though, and hoped that it just added more troops for him to capture; however, he wanted Arbuthnot to get control of the harbor and the Cooper River to prevent any further reinforcement or a possible escape.

On April 8, Arbuthnot made his attempt to sail into Charleston harbor. In the afternoon, the wind picked up and his eight warships and several transport ships moved toward Fort Moultrie. Inside the fort, Col. Charles Cotesworth Pinckney and the men of the 1st South Carolina prepared for a fight. One by one the British ships sailed to within 800 yards of the fort, and then past it and into the harbor. As they passed, the ships fired their cannons at the fort, and the fort returned the favor as thick white smoke filled the harbor around Sullivan's Island. But unlike the 1776 battle, the British did not stay and duke it out but quickly sped by. Each warship received enemy fire, but the damage for the most part was negligible. Within 90 minutes, all the ships had successfully

Gen. Benjamin Lincoln was in a difficult situation between preserving his army and defending the people and property of Charleston. (nypl)

A drawing depicting the skyline of Charleston in 1780. Note the Old Exchange Building and St. Michael's Church steeple. (nypl)

passed the fort except for one transport ship that ran aground and was abandoned. Overall, the British lost 27 men killed and wounded; the South Carolinians lost none. However, the British fleet was now in Charleston Harbor, anchored near Fort Johnson. A hope for a repeat of June 28, 1776, was lost. As soon as Arbuthnot's fleet captured the Cooper River, the city's fate would be sealed. The only thing stopping him was Whipple's small fleet of ships and the scuttled ships that the Americans placed near the entrance to the river to serve as an obstruction to the British fleet. These scuttled ships were sunk in a row and connected by cables to create a boom that ran from the Exchange Building in downtown Charleston to Shute's Folly in the Cooper River. This boom prevented British ships from entering the river and cutting off the city. But with the British fleet firmly in the harbor, now the British and the Hessians could celebrate as the tide had shifted in their favor.

The next day, April 9, the British had nearly completed their first parallel, and Clinton immediately ordered his men to begin digging approach trenches closer to the city. Lincoln's nearly 100 cannon continued firing on the British works, but with little effect. That evening, Arbuthnot came ashore to meet with Clinton and plan their reduction of Charleston.

On April 10, Clinton and Arbuthnot offered the city terms of surrender to avoid the "further effusion of blood." These terms were immediately rejected by Lincoln, who wrote that "Duty and inclination" required him to hold the town "to the last extremity."

On April 13, with artillery now mounted in the first parallel, the British opened fire on the American defenses. British cannon fire rained down on both the defensive lines and the city as the batteries on Fenwick's Point joined the cannonade. The American artillery returned fire and the entire peninsula was soon engulfed in smoke and flame. Among the projectiles fired into the town was "hot shot," which were cannon balls heated red hot so when they struck a wooden building it would catch it on fire.

During the day, as the city was bombarded, Lincoln convinced Governor John Rutledge and a few other members of the Privy Council that they should evacuate Charleston via the Cooper River opening. Lieutenant Governor Christopher Gadsden and five other members of the Privy Council would remain behind. Among those evacuated were the wounded

The approximate location on Ford Road of the battle of Biggin Bridge that occurred on April 14, 1780. (mm)

invalids, including Lt. Col. Francis Marion, who had injured his ankle the previous month. Marion's evacuation would prove to be especially important in the coming months as he took a leadership role in resistance to the British. Among the Continental officers remaining to direct the American defenses was Col. John Grimke. Grimke, a native South Carolinian, gained more notoriety in the future as the father of the Grimke sisters, who became famous abolitionists.

To preserve his escape route, avenue of supplies, and reinforcements along the Cooper and Wando Rivers, Lincoln fortified a position across the Cooper River at Lempriere's Point in Mount Pleasant, and then farther up the Wando at Cainhoy. Lincoln also dispatched his cavalry into that area. Some of the American cavalry were encamped at Biggin's Bridge near Monck's Corner (35 miles northeast of

These are 19th century Biggin Church ruins from a church built on the same site as the church during the Revolutionary War. (mm)

Charleston). Clinton sent Col. Banastre Tarleton and his legion to attack this outpost. Tarleton and his men made a surprise attack on the encampment in the early morning hours of April 14, 1780, routing the American cavalry and killing 15, wounding 18, and capturing 63, while losing only two men wounded. This destruction of the American cavalry opened the door for the British to advance east of the Cooper River and seal off the Patriots' only path of escape.

Now British soldiers freely roamed the countryside north and east of the city. Like those in the areas south and west, the civilian inhabitants suffered plunder and pillage as the invading troops marauded across the land. Depredations continued to affect the civilians with some very upsetting stories of plunder and rape. Mrs. Motte, wife of a Patriot colonel, was accosted by some British soldiers who were stealing the clothes off her children. She begged them to leave her baby alone, but instead they told her they wished the father was home so "they could rip his damned rebel heart out."

On April 13, the British began construction of a second parallel less than 300 yards from the American defenses of Charleston. The lines were within rifle range of each other, and the firing now included small arms. The British advance was slowed by increased fire from the Americans during this time. But the British were becoming very effective with their artillery, destroying and displacing much of the American artillery. Life in the British and American trenches became an increasingly dangerous occupation. With constant rifle and artillery fire, peering over one's respective entrenchments could bring about instant death. The casualties on both sides rose as the British inched closer to the city.

The men in the trenches on both sides had to deal with the unrelenting sun, heat, standing water, and mosquitos. As the British continued to inch closer, Ewald noted that the British were so close to the American lines that "one could easily throw a stone" into their fortifications. In addition to the arduous work in the trenches, death was a constant threat. Musket and rifle fire was very effective, and many men were killed just peering over their fortifications.

One of Moultrie's aides, Maj. Philip Neyle, was killed when a cannonball "took away part of his head." Colonel Richard Parker of Virginia, peering over the entrenchments, was shot in the head and

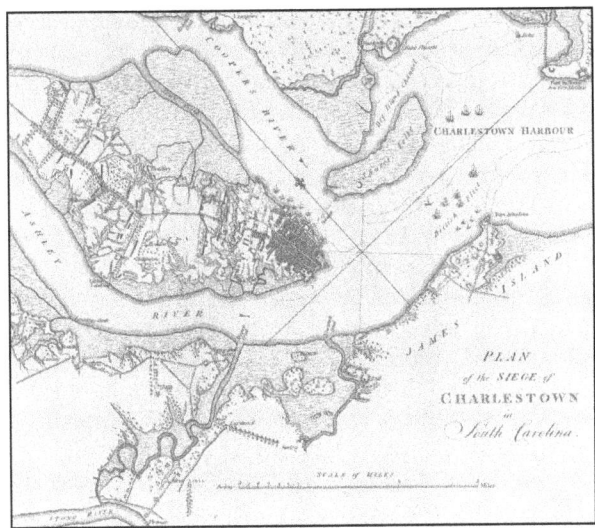

A plan of the siege of Charleston depicting the siege lines and the harbor. (nypl)

killed. Bullets whistled about as men like General Moultrie walked the lines.

Desertion was a major problem on both sides during this siege, but more so for the Americans. At one point, a British soldier deserted to the city, but after seeing the situation behind the American fortifications, three days later he deserted back to the British lines. The city was running very low on supplies, and both soldiers and civilians were running out of food.

As the British built the second parallel, south of the city, they constructed another battery on Stiles Point on James Island. This battery, like the one at Fenwick Point, was used primarily for shelling the city and not the defenses. British artillery from this position killed and wounded even more civilians. On April 16, a cannonball knocked off the arm of the statue of William Pitt, which stood at the intersection of Broad and Meeting Streets. A day later, a British cannonball flew into a house and killed a man and wounded a woman who were lying in bed. One Patriot major said, "the balls flew thro' the streets, and spent their fury on the houses." People were sent into a panic. Over the course of the siege, 20 civilians were killed, and 30 homes destroyed by British cannon fire.

On the morning of April 20, Lincoln held a council of war with his officers at his headquarters in the Hornwork. The Patriots were in a bind. They were outnumbered nearly two to one, their only escape route was nearly closed, and the Royal navy was poised to enter the Cooper River. With no word

The statue of William Pitt that once stood in the middle of Broad and Meeting Streets now stands in the Federal Judicial Court. Notice the arm missing that was taken off by a British cannonball during the siege. (mm)

A replica of the plaque that was affixed to the Pitt statue declares the esteem with which Charlestonians held this British politician who had stood up for their rights in Parliament. (mm)

of reinforcements on the way, Lincoln and his officers essentially had only two choices: evacuate the city and save the army to fight another day or surrender and request favorable terms. As they debated their options, Lieutenant Governor Gadsden joined them. He was dismayed to hear them having this discussion. The military officers adjourned and reassembled that evening with Gadsden and four members of the Privy Council. At this meeting, the civilian leaders were adamant that the army should stay. They were fearful that if the soldiers evacuated, the civilians would be left to endure the depredations of the invading army. The citizens of the city had already noticed that there were boats being collected in the Cooper River to facilitate the army's evacuation, and at least one member of the Privy Council noted that if they saw the army begin to evacuate that they would help the citizens turn on the Continental army, open the gates to the city, and let the British in. The military officers, realizing now that evacuation was all but impossible, agreed to continue to fight and hold out "to the last extremity."

The next morning, Lincoln sought a cease fire for six hours and told the British that he would surrender the city if certain terms were agreed upon. Among those terms was that the Continental army be allowed to march out from Charleston with their weapons to the central part of South Carolina. The British were furious that the rebels would even ask for such ludicrous terms and immediately rejected them. The ceasefire thus ended and both sides resumed heavy cannonading of each other. One British officer noted that "both the American & British lines seemed in a constant blaze."

By April 21, the British began construction of a third and final parallel just 800 feet from the American defenses. With the British closing in on the city, Lincoln attempted to strike and slow them down. In the early morning hours of April 24, 150 Americans under Col. William Henderson launched a sortie in which there was bloody hand-to-hand fighting near present-day Radcliffe and Coming Streets. Henderson's men charged into the British trenches with fixed bayonets, surprising the Hessian and British soldiers, who fought back furiously. During this brief engagement, 15 British soldiers were bayoneted and 12 taken prisoner. The Americans fell back to their lines having lost only three men. One of those, however, was General Moultrie's own brother, Capt. Thomas Moultrie.

The following night the British were so terrified of another sortie that when some of the men building the third parallel were fired upon by American soldiers, the work party retreated to the second parallel. In the darkness, and with all the confusion and fear, the British soldiers in the second line opened fire on the retreating troops, killing or wounding at least 20 of their own men.

Clinton was fearful that Lincoln would evacuate his army across the Cooper, and he desperately wanted to cut off this route of escape. He continued to pressure Arbuthnot to force his way into the Cooper River and had Gen. Charles Cornwallis command the troops he now sent over to the east side of the Cooper. Cornwallis immediately sent his men up the Wando River to intercept any American force that attempted to escape toward the north. Cornwallis also dispatched Colonel Tarleton's British Legion to ride around and collect forage and supplies but warned him to prevent his men from "committing irregularities." Despite these admonitions, the British soldiers continued to make life difficult for the civilians east of the Cooper River.

On April 26, Lincoln convened another council of war in Charleston to again consider their options. Evacuation was again deemed impossible and unwise, and they confirmed their determination to fight it out. That same day, Cornwallis's men marched down through Mount Pleasant and captured Haddrell's Point. The small American force there evacuated toward Fort Moultrie when they heard the British arrive. The Patriots now had only two fortified places east of the Cooper River: one garrison at Fort Moultrie and another at Lempriere's Point, with Cornwallis's force standing between them.

The next day, the garrison at Lempriere's Point, terrified that the British were going to assault them next, quickly and in a disorderly fashion evacuated their position and fell back across the Cooper River into Charleston. Cornwallis had believed the position too strong to assault, but with word that post was now empty, the British occupied it. This position was the key to keeping any communication or supply open to the rest of the state. With the British now firmly in control of Mount Pleasant, the fate of the American defenders was almost certainly sealed.

In Charleston, the British continued to fire on the city. Even though they were surrounded, the

A modern view from the area of Lempriere's Point looking towards Charleston and the Arthur Ravenel Jr. Bridge (built in 2005) that spans the Cooper River. (mm)

Americans were unwilling to surrender. Clinton was fearful he would be forced to launch an assault on the American position, a potentially risky and bloody affair. Lincoln, preparing for a British assault, decided to fully enclose the Hornwork. In the event a British assault pierced their lines, all the defenders would fall back to the Hornwork and fight to the last.

The British continued to construct the third parallel just a few hundred feet from the American defenses. The rifle fire was especially deadly as both sides effectively picked off men who looked over their lines. Work to repair sections of the defenses usually commenced at night as it was less likely the enemy could see those who labored on them. The defenders of Charleston, fearing a nighttime bayonet assault on their position, placed burning turpentine barrels in front of their works to illuminate the ground between the two opposing lines.

Clinton wanted to capture the dam on the Neck along the Cooper River that controlled the water flow in the canal in front of the American defenses. By May 1, the British soldiers and workers, under a hail of artillery and rifle fire, reached the dam and began to drain the canal.

As the British waited for the canal to drain, which would take a few days, they began to plan an assault on the city. Meanwhile, American cavalry and infantry were trying to rally in the back country to come to the city's defense. More Virginia Continentals under Col. Abraham Buford marched toward the city. However, on May 6, Tarleton surprised the American cavalry at Lenud's Ferry on the Santee River and charged into them. The Americans, taken completely by surprise, put up little resistance. Thirty Americans were cut down and more than 60 taken prisoner. Cornwallis believed this action "totally demolished" what remained of the American cavalry.

Back near Charleston, British troops landed on Sullivan's Island and marched toward Fort Moultrie and demanded the surrender of the fort and its 200 soldiers. The defenders refused, but when the British threatened to put them all to death, the Americans finally conceded. On May 7, Fort Moultrie, the site of the Patriots' great victory in 1776, fell to the British. More than anything, its capture was a major psychological blow to American morale.

On May 8, Clinton summoned Lincoln to surrender the garrison unconditionally. A ceasefire was called for one day as Lincoln and his officers negotiated with Clinton and Arbuthnot. Lincoln wanted the militia to be allowed to return home. He also wanted to protect civilian property, and to allow his army the dignity of flying their colors and beating their drums as they surrendered. Clinton refused

Tarleton totally destroyed the American cavalry at Lenud's Ferry on May 6, 1780. (mm)

and the ceasefire ended the next day, and that night some of the fiercest bombarding occurred. Both sides fired all night, and for a period the area along upper King Street must have seemed like hell itself. Moultrie remembered "There was a tremendous cannonade [180–200 pieces of heavy cannon firing], it was a glorious sight, to see them like meteors crossing each other, and bursting in the air; it appeared as if the stars were tumbling down. The fire was incessant almost the whole night; cannonballs whizzing and shells hissing continually amongst us; ammunition chests and temporary magazines blowing up, great guns bursting, and wounded men groaning along the lines: it was a dreadful night! It was our last great effort, but it availed us nothing."

Throughout the night and following day, the British inched closer and closer across the dry canal and now were just 20 yards from the American defenses. Inside those defenses, even though the Continentals were ready to continue to fight, the militia were exhausted and done. They essentially threw down their arms and petitioned Lincoln to surrender the city. The civilians also asked Lincoln to give up the fight. The two groups Lincoln was holding out to protect had essentially given up. On May 11, an American drummer and a man holding a white flag stood on top of the American defenses. Lincoln asked for a cessation of hostilities and agreed to surrender to the British under Clinton's previous terms. The siege of Charleston was over.

Walking Tour 3

This tour, designed as a walking tour, will focus on sites associated with the 1780 siege of Charleston and the occupied city. It starts at the first parallel on upper King Street and ends at the Battery in downtown Charleston, a distance of about two miles. This is a very long walk, so feel free to break it up as you see fit. But the best way to experience downtown Charleston is to wander the streets and closely explore the buildings and the history. Most of the historic homes are private residences, please respect the owners' privacy. Like the Freedom Trail in Boston, this long walk has numerous bars and restaurants along the way. Enjoy!

GPS: N 32.793036, W 79.941313

Tour Stop 1 — First Parallel

This is the location of the center of the British first parallel that was begun on April 1, 1780, just 800 yards from the main American defenses. You can see roughly where the American defenses were situated by looking south at the church steeple. Nothing remains of any of the British fortifications and nothing on the ground denotes the locations.

570 King St., Charleston, SC 29403
GPS: N 32.793036, W 79.941313

View from the site of the first parallel looking south toward the site of the American defenses near the church steeple in the distance. (mm)

→ TO TOUR STOP 2

Head south on King St. for 0.2 miles to the intersection of Mary/Morris St.

GPS: N 32.790515, W 79.939501

Tour Stop 2 – Second Parallel

You have arrived at the center of the British second parallel that was begun on April 13, 1780. This parallel was just 300 yards from the American lines. Again, the church steeple gives a good idea of the location of the American defensive lines. In addition to artillery fire, this parallel was within rifle shot, and casualties in both armies increased as the men engaged in routine firing.

513 King St., Charleston, SC 29403
GPS: N 32.790515, W 79.939501

View from the approximate site of the second parallel looking south. (mm)

→ TO TOUR STOP 3

Head south on King St. to the next block and turn right on Radcliffe St. Go two blocks to the intersection with Coming St.

GPS: N 32.788192, W 79.941298

Tour Stop 3 — Third Parallel

The British third parallel was attacked here by an American party on April 24, 1780. The third parallel, begun on April 21, 1780, was only 800 feet from the American lines, less than two blocks south of Coming Street. While the Hessians worked here in the early morning hours of April 24, Colonel Henderson and 150 men assaulted this position with fixed bayonets. The fighting was fierce, with 12 Hessians bayoneted in the hand-to-hand combat. William Moultrie's brother was killed in the fighting. There are no markers or interpretation here.

38 Radcliffe St., Charleston, SC 29403
GPS: N 32.788192, W 79.941298

View from the site of the third parallel looking south on King Street. (mm)

View from the site of the British third parallel that was attacked by Continentals commanded by Henderson. This view is from the British position looking south toward the American defenses. (mm)

⟫ TO TOUR STOP 4

Go one block south on Coming St. to the intersection with Warren St.

GPS: N 32.787327, W 79.940830

Tour Stop 4 — The Canal

This was the location of the Canal, a defensive waterway which ran across the peninsula and acted as a moat to prevent the British from assaulting the city. It was 18 feet wide and 8 feet deep. The water level was controlled on the east side by the Cooper River. To allow the Americans the ability to sortie across this canal, they placed planks across it to make temporary bridges. Once British troops captured the section on the east side, they slowly drained the canal to prepare for a possible infantry assault on the city. Today, you can see a small dip where this canal once ran on Elizabeth St.

52 Warren St, Charleston, SC 29403
GPS: N 32.787327, W 79.940830

⟫ TO TOUR STOP 5

Walk east on Warren St. for two blocks back onto King St. and turn right.

GPS: N 32.787796, W 79.937607

View looking east along the approximate length of where the canal once was that was part of the American defenses.
(mm)

Looking south along Elizabeth Street toward the American lines, a small dip in the road reveals the approximate location of the canal in this section of the defenses. (mm)

Tour Stop 5 – American Main Defensive Line

This was the location of the center of the main American defensive fortification. Here a large earthwork zigzagged across the peninsula. Just in front of this earthwork were abatis, or a tangle of wooden branches that acted like an early form of barbed wire. Between here and the British lines was a no man's land with no cover and pock marks from artillery shells. At night, burning turpentine barrels illuminated the ground. Constant firing with rifles, muskets, and artillery punctuated the air throughout the 42-day siege here. Most of the casualties during the siege occurred here on the main American line and in the British parallels just a few hundred yards away. There are no markers for this position.

423 King St., Charleston, SC 29403
GPS: N 32.787796, W 79.937607

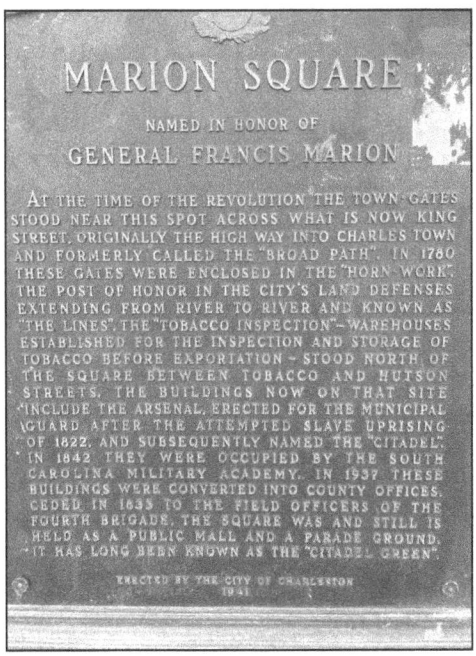

A plaque denotes the significance of Marion Square in Charleston. (mm)

TO TOUR STOP 6

Head south on King St. for one block to Marion Square.

GPS: N 32.786719, W 79.936492

Tour Stop 6 — The Hornwork

Marion Square, named for Francis Marion, was the location of the Hornwork and the center of the American defensive position during the Siege of Charleston. It later became the parade ground for the Citadel. The Citadel later moved to the west part of the city, but the old Citadel building still stands. (mm)

You are now at the location of the Hornwork. Just behind the main American line, this tabby redoubt was originally constructed during the French and Indian War in the 1750s and was improved during the 1780 siege. Additionally, it was enclosed to form a rallying position in the event the British pierced the American line. The entire Hornwork (along with the siege lines) was destroyed shortly after the war, and today only one small chunk of the fortification in Marion Square survives. Because it was destroyed so quickly after the war, many questions still exist as to how large it was and how tall and thick the walls were. We know it was large enough to hold a gate, while one French observer described its walls as being 30 feet tall. Lincoln made his headquarters in the Hornwork, and most of the

The only portion of the American defenses still visible is this small piece of tabby that has survived for more than 250 years. (mm)

major decisions regarding the American defense were made here as well. When the garrison surrendered, the formal ceremony occurred between the Hornwork and the main defensive line, where you just came from. Today, the only interpretation on site regarding the 1780 siege is the state historic marker you see on King Street in Marion Square. The erection of this marker was spearheaded by this author and supported by local heritage organizations and unveiled in 2010 on the 230th anniversary of the surrender.

A plaque on the fence around the remnant reads: "Remnant of Horn Work, Siege of Charleston, May 1780." (mm)

10 65
THE SIEGE OF
CHARLESTON, 1780

The British capture of
Charleston in May 1780 was
one of the worst American
defeats of the Revolution.
On March 30-31 Gen. Henry
Clinton's British, Hessian,
and Loyalist force crossed
the Ashley River north of
Charleston. On April 1
Clinton advanced against
the American defenses
near this site, held by
Gen. Benjamin Lincoln's
Continentals and militia.
The 42-day siege would be
the longest of the war.

The Surrender of Charleston

CHAPTER SEVEN

MAY 12, 1780

"This is the severest Blow We ever received."
— John Adams, June 24, 1780

Around noon on May 12, British and Hessian grenadiers entered the Hornwork and the British flag was raised over the American fortifications. The Continental army formed up, marched out of the fortifications, and laid down their weapons between their main defensive line and the Hornwork. Their flags were cased, and they were forced to play a Turkish march on their drums—an awful humiliation to the Patriot defenders. Charleston had officially fallen.

During the surrender ceremony, the British army watched the Continentals give up their arms. They were amazed to see the condition of the Americans and noted their clothes were ragged and torn, and many had no shoes. Yet they were extremely disciplined and professional. One British officer remarked it was "admirable that these people still fight for the chimerical freedom of America with such ardor." Many Continental soldiers were too sick to move, and some of the British expressed amazement that with so few men they had "made a gallant defense."

It was a costly siege. Over the course of 42 days, the Americans lost 89 men killed and 138 wounded. The British lost 99 killed and 217 wounded. The British were successful in capturing the city, but more importantly, they captured the Americans' entire southern army: 5,618 men, 400 cannon, 15 stands of flags, and 5,000 muskets. Of the men captured, 3,465 were hardened veteran regulars who were irreplaceable to the Americans. In one swoop, the Continental lines

The Siege of Charleston was the biggest defeat America experienced in the Revolutionary War. Though often overlooked, the battlefield lies just below the surface in the historic city. This historic marker was erected in Marion Square near the scene of the surrender in 2010. (mm)

The British flag flutters over Fort Moultrie during a reenactment of the British occupation in 2010. (mm)

of Virginia, North Carolina, and South Carolina ceased to exist. Among the prisoners were three signers of the Declaration of Independence: Arthur Middleton, Edward Rutledge and Thomas Heyward. The militia would be allowed to go home on parole, but the Continentals would be retained in the city as prisoners. This was the largest defeat the American cause suffered during the Revolutionary War. The next time that an American army surrendered a

British reenactors raise the British flag over Fort Moultrie during a reenactment in 2010. (mm)

larger force to a foreign enemy was at Bataan in World War II.

All the weapons and ammunition were gathered by the British to be placed in arsenals for use by the British or Loyalists. But this simple task resulted in a tragedy because some of the weapons were loaded and were being handled roughly. On May 15, 1780, a British soldier carelessly tossed some muskets into one of the arsenals that also contained 4,000 pounds of black powder. One of the muskets accidentally discharged, causing a horrific explosion that rocked the entire city. Soldiers and civilians standing nearby were killed instantly. Moultrie noted that these victims' "carcasses, legs, and arms were seen in the air, and scattered over several parts of the town."

The approximate location on King Street where the gate of the Hornwork was located. (mm)

The Americans laid down their arms, just outside the walls of the Hornwork, about in the location where the old Citadel building stands on Marion Square. (mm)

An image from the approximate location of the powder magazine that exploded on May 15, 1780, on Magazine Street looking towards St. John's Church. (mm)

He graphically described "one man was dashed with violence against the steeple of the new independent church [modern Unitarian Church], which was at a great distance from the explosion, and left the marks of his body there for several days." Swords and bayonets rained down on the houses all around. Men, both American and British, who ran to put out the inferno, had to take cover as other loaded muskets fired randomly. All in all, almost 200 people were killed in the blast (more than lost in the entire siege) and at least six buildings were razed, including a poorhouse, a brothel, and a nearby prison. Ewald, even as a hardened veteran, never "witnessed a more deplorable sight." He too "found some sixty people who were burnt beyond recognition, half-dead and writhing like worms," and saw "a number of mutilated bodies hanging on the farthest houses and lying in the streets." At first, many British and Hessian soldiers

At the Waxhaws, a relief column of Virginia troops that had been on the way to Charleston was chased down by Banastre Tarleton and more than a hundred men were killed. (nypl)

THE BATTLE OF THE WAXHAWS, MAY 29TH, 1780.

thought this was an act of sabotage by the Americans, but it was ultimately determined to have simply been a tragic accident.

The British now possessed the wealthy and strategic port city of Charleston. As they solidified their occupation of the city, Clinton dispatched Cornwallis to subdue the South Carolina countryside. A small detachment of some 300 Virginia Continentals under the command of Col. Abraham Buford was marching to join Lincoln at Charleston when news reached them of the fall of the city. Buford's men, who had made it to the Santee River, turned and headed back north. Cornwallis sent Tarleton's Legion after them. When Tarleton caught up with Buford at the Waxhaws near the North Carolina border on May 29, his men charged into the Virginians. The one-sided action resulted in 113 Virginians killed and more than 150 severely wounded. Tarleton's command suffered only 5 killed and 12 wounded. The event became known as the Waxhaws Massacre. The brutality of Tarleton's troops would serve as a rallying cry for Patriots throughout the backcountry over the following months.

In June 1780, Clinton left Charleston and returned to the main British army in New York City, leaving Cornwallis in command in South Carolina. Cornwallis was left with the unenviable task of trying to get the rest of the state under control. But contrary to what they believed; no major uprising of Loyalists materialized in the aftermath of the grand British victory at Charleston. Instead, what ensued over the following two years was a bloody civil war fought throughout the backcountry of South Carolina. Marching into the wilderness to subdue the Patriots in the interior of the state, Cornwallis met with initial success, but his efforts eventually failed, leading to

Banastre Tarleton commanded a legion of American Loyalists called the British Legion. They became renowned for their effectiveness and brutality. Following the engagement at Waxhaws, giving no quarter for wounded or surrendering troops became known derisively as "Tarleton's Quarter." (nypl)

A marker on the Waxhaws battlefield. The battle is often referred to as the Waxhaws Massacre or Buford's Massacre. (mm)

A marker denotes the location of a mass grave of Continental soldiers at the Waxhaws battlefield. (mm)

total defeat at Yorktown, Virginia, in October 1781. The road to Yorktown began at Charleston in May 1780.

➤ TO TOUR STOP 7

Head South on King St. to Calhoun St. Turn right on Calhoun St. Go past St. Phillip St. and turn left into the Cougar Mall on the College of Charleston campus. Walking past the marker to Andrew Jackson's mother will bring you to the rear of Randolph Hall. Walk around to the front of Randolph Hall.

GPS: N 32.784461, W 79.937696

Tour Stop 7 – The Colonial Barracks

This was the location of the Barracks in Charleston. Today it is the College of Charleston. The College of Charleston was founded in 1770 but did not hold classes here until after the Revolutionary War. The main campus building was not constructed until the 19th century. At the time of the Revolutionary War there were two large rectangular brick buildings at this location that served as barracks for the Patriots. After the city surrendered, many of the thousands of Continental soldiers were held in these barracks as prisoners of war. Today, a marker on the library building shows the two bricks that remain from these colonial buildings. There is a marker to Andrew Jackson's mother, Elizabeth Hutchinson Jackson, who volunteered to help sick prisoners during a cholera outbreak in November 1781. While caring for the sick, she contracted the disease and died, leaving 14-year-old Andrew an orphan. The college also played a role as a filming location for the movie *The Patriot* in 2000.

66 George St., Charleston, SC 29424
GPS: N 32.784461, W 79.937696

 **TO TOUR STOP 8**

Head south to George St. and turn left. Turn right onto St. Phillip St. Go past Wentworth St. and make a slight right onto Archdale St. Continue south on Archdale St. to Magazine St. Turn right onto Magazine St. and walk halfway down the block.

GPS: N 32.778849, W 79.935482

This marker on the campus of the College of Charleston denotes the approximate location of the grave of Elizabeth Jackson, Andrew Jackson's mother. She died of smallpox while administering to the sick and wounded Continental soldiers in Charleston in November of 1781. (mm)

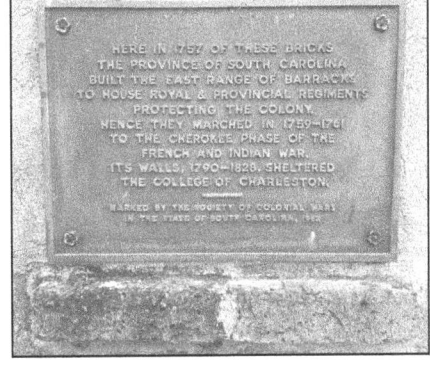

This small marker on the southeast corner of Towell Library on the campus of the College of Charleston contains the only two bricks remaining of the barracks that once stood on this location during the Revolutionary War. (mm)

Tour Stop 8 — The Explosion Site

Though nothing is left today, this was the location of the powder magazine that exploded on May 15, 1780. The blast killed more people than had died in combat on the peninsula during the siege. In addition to killing the guards and civilians, the explosion destroyed a nearby jail and school.

2 Magazine St, Charleston, SC 29401
GPS: N 32.778849, W 79.935482

▶ TO TOUR STOP 9

Go back to Archdale St. and turn right. You will see the church to your left.

GPS: N 32.778565, W 79.934350

The steeple on the Unitarian Church dates to the nineteenth century, but the steeple on the church in 1780 was the one that William Moultrie noted that a person was dashed against during the explosion of the powder magazine. (mm)

Tour Stop 9 – Unitarian Church and Graveyard

This was the site of "Independent Church" in 1780. Today it is the Unitarian church. The building has been greatly altered but sits on the same site. This was the church where in 1780 a body was catapulted onto its steeple by the arsenal explosion, leaving an imprint for days. The church was still under construction during the war, and while the British occupied Charleston, they stabled some of their horses here. The church graveyard is truly unique in that it is purposefully overgrown, adding a romantic and wild feel to the site. Buried here is one citizen who was captured at the siege and sent to St. Augustine, Florida, Jonathan Daniel Héctor de Saussure.

4 Archdale St., Charleston, SC 29401
GPS: N 32.778565, W 79.934350

▷ TO TOUR STOP 10

Turn around on Archdale St. and go north to Clifford St. Turn right onto Clifford St. Continue walking straight across King St. and Meeting St. as the road changes names from Clifford St. to

The graveyard at the Unitarian Church is one of the most interesting and romantic in the city. Jonathan Daniel Héctor de Saussure, a citizen who was sent to St. Augustine in 1780, is buried here. (mm)

Horlbeck Alley to Cumberland St. Before reaching Church St., you will see the Powder Magazine on your right.

GPS: N 32.779548, W 79.930119

Tour Stop 10 – The Powder Magazine

This is the location of the colonial-era powder magazine. Dating back to 1713, it's the oldest public building in South Carolina. During the siege of Charleston, Moultrie moved much of the powder from this magazine to the Old Exchange Building to protect it from being hit by artillery fire. Today the building is owned by the Colonial Dames and is operated as a museum interpreting the history of colonial Charleston.

The Powder Magazine is the oldest public building in Charleston and is operated as a museum of colonial history by the Colonial Dames. (mm)

79 Cumberland St., Charleston, SC 29401
GPS: N 32.779548, W 79.930119

➤ TO TOUR STOP 11

Leaving the Powder Magazine, turn right onto Cumberland St., and then immediately turn right onto Church St., where you will see St. Philip's Church.

GPS: N 32.778967, W 79.929500

Tour Stop 11 — St. Philip's Church

The church you see here today was built in 1836. However, the parish dates to 1681 and a different church building stood on this site during the Revolutionary War. Buried in the cemetery are numerous prominent figures of Revolutionary War Charleston, including Christopher Gadsden, Charles Pinckney, and Edward Rutledge.

142 Church St., Charleston, SC 29401
GPS: N 32.778967, W 79.929500

➤ TO TOUR STOP 12

Continue south on Church St. to the next block, Queen St. Turn right onto Queen St. Go two blocks to King St. and then turn left. Go one block to Broad St. and turn right. The John Rutledge House will be on your right.

GPS: N 32.776561, W 79.933322

The congregation at St. Philip's Church has worshiped at this site since 1723. The steeple (finished in 1850) leans slightly due to multiple Union cannonballs that struck it during the Civil War and a major earthquake that struck Charleston in 1886. (mm)

Tour Stop 12 – John Rutledge House

The home of Governor John Rutledge is original, though the ornate ironwork on the front of the building was added later in the 19th century. It was in this home that the Privy Council met on May 11, 1779, and where Rutledge suggested offering South Carolina's neutrality. In 1791, George Washington had breakfast here. Across Broad St. is the home of Edward Rutledge, John's brother and a signer of the Declaration of Independence. Today, both homes are operated as bed and breakfasts.

116 Broad St., Charleston, SC 29401
(N 32.776561, W 79.933322)

➡ TO TOUR STOP 13

Head east on Broad St. for one block to St. Michael's Church.

GPS: N 32.776388, W 79.930995

Tour Stop 13 – St. Michaels Church

St. Michael's Church is the oldest church building in Charleston, dating to 1761. The steeple you see would have been familiar to all those in Revolutionary War-era Charleston. During the siege of Charleston in 1780, a Patriot, Peter Timothy, stayed up in the steeple and kept an eye on the approaching British Army. In 1791, George Washington worshipped here and climbed the steeple to take in the view of Charleston. In the graveyard are the final resting places of John Rutledge, Charles Cotesworth Pinckney, and the Marylander Mordecai Gist.

71 Broad St., Charleston, SC 29401
GPS: N 32.776388, W 79.930995

➡ TO TOUR STOP 14

Stand near the intersection of Broad St. and Meeting St.

GPS: N 32.776590, W 79.931313

A carriage tour drives past St. Michael's Church. (mm)

Tour Stop 14 — The Four Corners of Law

This intersection of Broad Street and Meeting Street is known as the Four Corners of Law. On the southeast corner is St. Michael's Church, on the southwest corner the United States Post Office and Federal Courthouse, on the northeast corner the City Hall building, and on the northwest corner the Charleston County Courthouse (the state capitol building during the 18th century). Thus, in this one intersection, you can see representations of the law of the federal, state, and local governments and the law of God. The Charleston County Courthouse originally dates to 1753, when it was the state house. A fire gutted the interior in 1788 and it was rebuilt in 1792, likely with the aid of Irish-born architect James Hoban. When George Washington visited in 1791, he saw its construction and later recruited Hoban to design the United States White House in

The colonial State House and current Charleston County Courthouse. (mm)

Washington, D.C. Inside the City Hall building is a large portrait of George Washington done by John Trumbull. It was commissioned by the city following Washington's visit. Behind the City Hall building is Washington Square Park, where a statue of George Washington stands, also commemorating his 1791 visit. Inside the Charleston County Judicial Center you can find the statue of William Pitt that during the Revolutionary War stood in the middle of the intersection of Broad and Meeting Streets. You will notice his right arm is missing, the victim of a British cannonball during the siege of Charleston in 1780.

84 Broad St., Charleston, SC 29401
GPS: N 32.776590, W 79.931313

 TO TOUR STOP 15

Continue east on Broad St for two blocks to the Old Exchange Building.

GPS: N 32.776840, W 79.926920

Tour Stop 15 — Old Exchange Building

Perhaps the most historic building in Charleston, it was finished in 1771 and served as the custom house for the city. In 1774, during protests against the tea tax, confiscated British tea was stored here. During the siege of Charleston, Moultrie moved the black powder from the powder magazine to this building and bricked it up to keep it safe. When the British army occupied the building, the basement was turned into a prison for American Patriots. Among those imprisoned was Isaac Hayne while he awaited execution. After the Americans liberated the city in 1782, the black powder was found behind the brick wall, the British never realizing that the supplies were hidden literally beneath their feet. In 1791, George Washington was lavishly entertained in this building.

122 E Bay St., Charleston, SC 29401
GPS: N 32.776840, W 79.926920

The Old Exchange building in Charleston is one of the most historic buildings in the city and today is operated as a museum by the city. (mm)

Occupied Charleston

CHAPTER EIGHT

1780–1782

"The British, in violation of their solemn compact, put [the Continental soldiers] on board of prison-ships."

— Dr. Peter Fayssoux

Charleston was now securely in British hands, and Cornwallis set up his headquarters in town. While a few hundred Loyalists were pleased with the British success, most Charlestonians were either in favor of the Patriot cause or merely trying to survive this tumultuous time. The British turned their efforts to subduing the rest of the state of South Carolina but were now also in charge of administering Charleston as well as feeding, caring for, and guarding thousands of prisoners. The city was placed under martial law.

Immediately after surrendering, the Continental soldiers were imprisoned within the city, mostly at the Barracks. The militia were paroled after giving their word they would no longer take up arms in the conflict. Many of them left the city and, unsurprisingly, broke their parole and joined the Patriot militias in the backcountry.

The British, fearful that the Continental officers would encourage the prisoners to revolt against their captors, separated them from their men. The Continental officers were sent across the Cooper River to Haddrell's Point and Mount Pleasant. General William Moultrie and Col. Charles Cotesworth Pinckney were quartered at Snee Farm. The officers were given fairly good treatment and afforded a large degree of freedom of movement in the area. Some, though, such as Gen. William Woodford, died of disease.

The Miles Brewton House was used as British headquarters after the city surrendered. It was later used as Union headquarters during the American Civil War in 1865.
(mm)

Snee Farm is where William Moultrie stayed as a prisoner of war. The plantation was the country retreat of Charles Pinckney. Pinckney served as an officer in the South Carolina militia and was captured during the Siege of Charleston in 1780. He went on to be a delegate to the Constitutional Convention and George Washington had breakfast here in 1791. Today the plantation is maintained by the National Park Service as the Charles Pinckney National Historic Site. (mm)

Additionally, to keep the Revolutionary leaders separated from the populace in Charleston, many civilian leaders were exiled. At first, most of the civilian leaders who were in Charleston during the siege were made prisoners but were released on parole, and many stayed in the city. However, later in the summer of 1780, the British decided to round up these men and exile them to St. Augustine, Florida, where a large fort, the Castillo San Marcos, was located. Among the exiled were Christopher Gadsden, the remaining members of the Privy Council, judges and other officials, and three signers of the Declaration of Independence: Edward Rutledge, Thomas Heyward, Jr., and Arthur Middleton. Like the officers, these men, though prisoners, had a decent accommodation. But the opposite was true for the common soldiers who surrendered at Charleston.

In the weeks following the surrender, the British faced a real problem: Continental prisoners escaping. Since the Barracks were not very far from defensive lines, many prisoners saw an excellent opportunity to make their escape from Charleston. Successful breakouts became such a problem that in August 1780, the British took the drastic step of moving many of the captives to prison ships in Charleston harbor.

Employing prison ships was not new for the British army, since they used them in New York Harbor for the previous four years. The old ships were turned into floating hulks where escape was much more difficult. But with hundreds of prisoners crammed on the ships, filth and disease were rampant.

The Continental officers were held at Haddrell's Point in Mount Pleasant. (nypl)

Feeding, guarding, and caring for these prisoners was an unenviable task, and the British were eager to exchange them for their own captured at the battle of Saratoga. But the Americans were wary of having those British combatants back in the conflict. As prisoner negotiations went nowhere, the sick season descended upon Charleston that fall. With mosquitoes and fevers rampant, the death toll rose higher and higher on the prison ships. As men died, their bodies were simply tossed overboard into the water below. To add to the misery, following the crushing American

The Castillo de San Marcos in St. Augustine, Florida. (mm)

Thomas Heyward, Jr. was a signer of the Declaration of Independence who was captured at the Siege of Charleston. His residence was later used by George Washington during his visit to Charleston in 1791. (nypl)

Edward Rutledge, the brother of John Rutledge, signed the Declaration of Independence and was captured in Charleston in 1780. His home sits across the street from John Rutledge's home on Broad Street. (nypl)

defeat at the battle of Camden in August of 1780, hundreds more prisoners entered the Charleston prison ships.

Eager to be relieved of having to care for the men, the British soon allowed American prisoners to enlist in the British Army. Former Royal Governor of South Carolina Lord Charles Greville Montagu recruited an entire regiment of soldiers from the prison ships for service in the West Indies. The regiment was named The Duke of Cumberland's Regiment, and they were promised they would fight French and Spanish enemies and not their American brethren. Many prisoners needed little prodding to take an opportunity to escape the hell on the prison ships, but many men refused to sell out their country or cause and later paid the ultimate price for their convictions.

Moultrie remembered one day in January 1781 when the British had the few American prisoners remaining in the Barracks marched out and given an ultimatum: join the British army or be moved to a prison ship, depriving their families of any rations. "Human nature recoiled from so horrid a declaration . . . for a few seconds the unhappy victims seemed stupefied at the dreadful prospect; a gloomy and universal silence prevailed . . . This was followed by a loud huzzah for General Washington, death and the prison ships was the unanimous determination." What drove these Continentals to suffer such hell we may never know, but clearly these men sacrificed for their country.

Montagu went further than trying to convince the common soldiers to join the British. He even reached out to his old friend General Moultrie to see if he would like to desert to the British. Moultrie was furious at the offer and rejected it outright. He wrote to Montagu that he had joined the Patriot side "with a determined resolution to risque my life and fortune in the cause" and that "I shall continue to go on as I have begun, that my example may encourage the youths of America to stand forth in defence of their rights and liberties … Good God! Is it possible that such an idea could arise in the breast of a man of honor?"

By the summer of 1781, as Cornwallis and his army were marching toward Virginia, the British and American leaders finally agreed on a prisoner exchange, and in June, the 750 remaining Continental prisoners in Charleston were sent to Virginia to be exchanged. These 750 were all that were left from the nearly 4,000 Americans captured at Charleston and Camden. Of these, more than 850 enlisted in the British Army, a few hundred were impressed in the Royal navy, nearly 1,000 had escaped, and more than 800 perished of disease or wounds on the prison ships.

As the men and civilians suffered under British military rule in Charleston, the theater of war moved into the Carolina backcountry. John Rutledge, who had successfully fled Charleston, was actively trying to raise more militia and acted as the single civilian authority for the state of South Carolina.

After routing the American army at Camden in August 1780, Cornwallis continued his campaign to stamp out Patriot resistance. A bloody partisan war broke out all across the state as men such as Francis Marion, Thomas Sumter, and Andrew Pickens operated a *petite guerre*, attacking British supply lines and outposts. Cornwallis tried to use the cavalry he had under Tarleton to defeat these Patriots, but the effort ended in failure. Loyalist militias also engaged in combat, turning the Carolina countryside into the scene of a brutal civil war. In October 1780, a bloody battle took place at Kings Mountain in South Carolina, where the rank and file soldiers on both sides were all Americans. The Patriot victory there helped to turn the tide in the Southern Theater.

In November 1780, Washington sent Gen. Nathanael Greene to take command of the Southern Department of the Continental army. Once in South Carolina, Greene sent Gen. Daniel Morgan and part of his army out into the western part of South Carolina, and a force under Tarleton gave chase.

Arthur Middleton signed the Declaration of Independence and was captured by the British at the Siege of Charleston in 1780. (nypl)

The HMS *Jersey* was the most notorious prison ship during the Revolutionary War. It was anchored in New York Harbor, but in Charleston Harbor, similar ships were used to hold American prisoners of war. (nypl)

On January 17, 1781, Morgan's force destroyed Tarleton's detachment at the battle of Cowpens. A furious Cornwallis chased Greene's army throughout the backcountry, finally encountering the Americans at Guilford Courthouse on March 15. Though Cornwallis won this battle, he lost nearly a third of his army. Cornwallis's battered force moved east and eventually north into Virginia at Yorktown. While Cornwallis moved to Virginia, Greene continued to fight in South Carolina and push the British back into Charleston.

In that summer of 1781, a tragic story unfolded in the city of Charleston. After the fall of Charleston, a South Carolina militia officer, Col. Isaac Hayne, had voluntarily entered the British lines to get medicine for his family, who were suffering from smallpox. While there, he was forced to sign an oath of allegiance to the British Crown, or else be held as a prisoner. Under duress, and under a gentleman's agreement with Brig. Gen. James Patterson, the Commandant of Charleston, that he would not have to serve against his fellow citizens, Hayne left the city as a prisoner on parole. By the summer of 1781, as the British pulled back toward Charleston, Hayne rejoined the Patriot militia. In July, after a brief clash with some Loyalist militia, Hayne was captured and sent to Charleston where he was imprisoned in the Old Exchange Building. The British, wanting to make an example of men breaking their paroles (and frustrated as the tide of war shifted) made the decision to have Hayne hanged for espionage. He was given no trial. The date of execution was moved back a few days so his children could visit him at the Old Exchange, and on

IN MEMORY OF
ELIZABETH HUTCHINSON
JACKSON
MOTHER OF
ANDREW JACKSON
PRESIDENT OF THE U.S. 1829–1837
WHO GAVE HER LIFE IN THE
CAUSE OF INDEPENDENCE
WHILE NURSING REVOLUTIONARY
SOLDIERS IN CHARLES TOWN
AND IS BURIED IN CHARLESTON
ERECTED BY
REBECCA MOTTE CHAPTER D.A.R.

Another marker honoring the sacrifice of Elizabeth Jackson can be found in Washington Square behind City Hall. (mm)

August 4, 1781, Hayne was taken to a site just outside the city fortifications and hanged. The decision to execute Hayne outraged the Patriots and Congress. Greene debated executing a random British officer in retaliation, but never did. However, the public perception of this cruel act inspired many to join the Patriot side in the last few months of the war.

Though the British, now under command of Lord Rawdon, continued to cede ground to Greene's army in South Carolina, they continued to win tactical victories. However, they could not control the countryside nor destroy Greene's army. Major battles occurred at Ninety-Six, Hobkirk Hill, and Eutaw Springs. After the bloody battle of Eutaw Springs, the British pulled all the way back to Charleston.

As Greene fought these battles in South Carolina, Washington moved most of his army in New York south to Virginia where he and a French fleet ultimately captured Cornwallis and his army of nearly 8,000 soldiers at Yorktown. Washington, keenly aware of how the Continentals were treated at the surrender of Charleston, gave the same terms to Cornwallis; the army was denied the right to march out with their flags flying, the normal honors for an army that fought honorably. When Cornwallis's second in command, Charles O'Hara, went forward to surrender his sword, he first offered it to the French commander, Comte de Rochambeau, who insisted it go to Washington. Washington in turn refused and insisted it go to the man who had surrendered Charleston, Gen. Benjamin Lincoln. The battle of Yorktown proved to be the ultimate decisive victory of the war.

While the major combat of the war was all but over, and as peace commissioners planned to meet in Paris to officially end the war, battles were still being

British soldiers routinely gave American prisoners opportunities to defect to the British side. While some took this option, many others stayed and often paid the ultimate price for their convictions. (loc)

View from the site of the encampment of Greene's army in 1782, Ashley Hill plantation. Today it is the location of the Middleton Inn, adjacent to Middleton Place Plantation. (mm)

fought in South Carolina. In the backcountry, Loyalist and Patriot militias engaged each other in numerous small actions. Around Charleston, small engagements and raids occurred between the Patriot soldiers and the British still occupying the city. Though these engagements were small and largely inconsequential, men were still fighting and dying. In one of the most tragic engagements, a small group of Patriots attacked some British soldiers at Tar Bluff along the Combahee River. The Patriots were led by the intrepid Lt. Col. John Laurens, who had recently played a conspicuous role in the capture of the British at Yorktown. Laurens, always rash and eager to achieve military glory, led in the front of his small detachment of men as they attacked the British line on August 27, 1782. The redcoats opened fire on the attackers and a musket ball struck Laurens in the head and killed him instantly. Both George Washington and Alexander Hamilton were devastated by the loss of so important an officer. Laurens likely would have played a major role in the creation of the new government, but we will never know. His young life was snuffed out at Tar Bluff in a needless skirmish.

As summer turned to winter in 1782, Greene and his army awaited the evacuation of Charleston while encamped at Ashley Hill plantation, just 20 miles from Charleston near Middleton Place plantation. Keeping his starving men together was no easy task, but he was able to hang on despite many of them deserting or dying from disease. Deaths from disease were especially numerous that fall. Colonel Josiah Harmer wrote in September 1782 that "in the course of this month we have buried near one hundred men." Over the course of the fall, more than 200 of Greene's men perished at Ashley Hill. The deaths became so frequent that Greene eventually forbade the death march being played at funerals as it became too commonplace. The stench from the sick and dying was overwhelming to visitors. When William Moultrie visited the camp, he noted that "the air was so infected with the stench of the camp, that we could scarcely bear the smell." Greene was desperate for the British to evacuate, and somehow kept the Continental army together at this trying time.

One small battle marked the last blood spilled in the Revolutionary War in South Carolina. On November 14, 1782, a small group of Marylanders under the command of Col. Thaddeus Kosciusko attacked a contingent of British troops who were foraging on James Island. A brief firefight erupted in what would be called the battle of Dills Bluff. Among the killed was the man often remembered as being the final fatality of the Revolutionary War, Capt. William Wilmot of the 2nd Maryland regiment. A war that broke out on Lexington Green in Massachusetts in April 1775 saw its last death on James Island. Other naval battles between Great Britain and France would occur around the globe through 1783, but the war in America was over.

This marker notes the location of the final action in South Carolina of the Revolutionary War in November of 1782. (mm)

The British finally decided that they would pull all their men out of Charleston in December. They communicated their intention to General Greene and pledged if they were not harassed by American troops, they would not destroy the property and buildings of the city. They set December 14, 1782, as the evacuation day.

▶ TO TOUR STOP 16

Walk north on East Bay St. to Vendue Range and turn right. Follow Vendue Range to the park and pier at the end of the street.

GPS: N 32.779020, W 79.925125

Tour Stop 16 – Waterfront Park

At Waterfront Park, you can get a good view of the harbor. Near the pier you can also see some metal maps depicting the historic growth on the peninsula. Across the Cooper River, you can see Haddrell's Point and Mount Pleasant. In the middle of the river, you can see Shute's Folly and the 19th-century fortification of Castle Pinckney. During the siege of Charleston in 1780, a boom and numerous obstructions blocked the river from the Exchange building to Shute's Folly.

Vendue Range, Concord St.,
Charleston, SC 29401
GPS: N 32.779020, W 79.925125

Waterfront Park in Charleston, near the historic location of Prioleau's Wharf. (mm)

Metal plaques show the growth of the city over time at Waterfront Park, the historic location of Prioleau's Wharf.
(mm)

⟹ TO TOUR STOP 17

Head back up Vendue Range to East Bay St. and turn left. Halfway down the block on the right side is Unity Alley and the location of McCrady's Tavern.

GPS: N 32.778276, W 79.927181

Tour Stop 17 – McCrady's Tavern

This building was Edward McCrady's tavern. The building dates to 1778. By 1788, he had completed his Long Room, and in 1791 this was the site of a large gala event for George Washington, hosted by the local Society of the Cincinnati.

155 E Bay St., Charleston, SC 29401
GPS: N 32.778276, W 79.927181

⟹ TO TOUR STOP 18

Walk through Unity Alley to State St. and turn left. Walk to Chalmers St. and turn right. Walk to Church St. and turn left.

Follow Church St. south for three blocks and the Heyward-Washington House will be on your right.

GPS: N 32.775294, W 79.929137

Tour Stop 18 — Heyward-Washington House

This was the home of signer of the Declaration of Independence Thomas Heyward, who was captured at the siege of Charleston. The house was finished in 1772, and in 1791 George Washington stayed here during his 10-day visit to the city. Today, it is operated as a historic house museum by The Charleston Museum.

87 Church St., Charleston, SC 29403
GPS: N 32.775294, W 79.929137

▶ TO TOUR STOP 19

Continue south on Church St. and turn right onto Tradd St. Go two and a half blocks down Tradd St.

GPS: N 32.774407, W 79.933327

Tour Stop 19 — John Stuart House

Built in 1772, this was the home of Col. John Stuart. Stuart was a Loyalist who ended up dying in Florida during the war. His home was confiscated by Patriots, and it was in this house that according to legend, some continental officers were enjoying many alcoholic drinks during the siege of Charleston. Francis Marion, who did not drink, attempted to leave but the doors had been locked. To escape the party, he jumped out of the window and into the street, breaking his ankle. This event saved Marion from being captured in May 1780, and may have helped the cause of American independence, as he would play an important role in wresting South Carolina from the British.

106 Tradd St., Charleston, SC 29401
GPS: N 32.774407, W 79.933327

The John Stuart House was the location where Francis Marion supposedly broke his ankle by jumping out the window. This resulted in him being evacuated from the city and ensuring he could fight another day. (mm)

➤ TO TOUR STOP 20

Head east on Tradd St. to King St. Turn right onto King St. Follow King St. south to the intersection with Ladson St.

GPS: N 32.772399, W 79.932247

Tour Stop 20 – Miles Brewton House

This house was built in 1769. Miles Brewton was a wealthy and prominent citizen in Charleston, and in 1775 was elected to the Second Continental Congress. However, his ship sank, and he was lost at sea while sailing to Philadelphia. During the British occupation of the city between 1780 and 1782, his home was used as Clinton's, Cornwallis's, and Lord Rawdon's headquarters.

27 King St., Charleston, SC 29401
GPS: N 32.772399, W 79.932247

After Miles Brewton died at sea, the house was left to his sister, Rebecca Brewton Motte, an avowed Patriot, who played an important role in the Siege of Fort Motte in May of 1781. (mm)

▶ TO TOUR STOP 21

Follow Ladson St. to Meeting St.

GPS: N 32.772815, W 79.930540

Tour Stop 21 – Royal Governor's House

You are now standing at home of Lord William Campbell, the last royal governor of South Carolina. In 1775, fearing for his life, Campbell fled from this home to a British warship. He later took part in the attack on Sullivan's Island and ultimately died from wounds he suffered there.

34 Meeting St., Charleston, SC 29401
GPS: N 32.772815, W 79.930540

This was the home from which the Royal Governor of South Carolina fled in 1775. (mm)

This was the home of William Washington after the Revolutionary War. (mm)

TO TOUR STOP 22

Head south on Meeting St. to Atlantic St. Turn left onto Atlantic St. Turn right onto Church St. and head to the end of the street.

GPS: N 32.770250, W 79.929621

Tour Stop 22 — William Washington House

This was the post-war home of William Washington. William was a distant cousin of George Washington and was wounded at the battle of Trenton in 1776. Later, he was sent south and commanded cavalry throughout South Carolina, playing important roles in many battles including Cowpens. He was wounded and captured at the battle of Eutaw Springs. After the war, he settled in Charleston and acquired this home in 1785. The building dates to before the Revolutionary War. William lived in Charleston until his death in 1810 and is today buried nearby in Rantowles, South Carolina.

3 Church St., Charleston, SC 29401
GPS: N 32.770250, W 79.929621

Charleston Liberated

CHAPTER NINE

DECEMBER 14, 1782

"I have the honor to communicate to your Excellency the agreeable information of the evacuation of Charles Town . . ."

— Gen. Nathanael Greene to Gen. George
Washington, Dec. 19, 1782

On the morning of December 14, 1782, the British loaded their ships on the Cooper River. As the British and Hessian soldiers boarded, thousands of Loyalists and slaves joined them. General "Mad" Anthony Wayne and a few hundred soldiers along with 80 men of Lee's Legion marched down King Street toward the city. Behind them was the rest of the American army with the new governor of South Carolina, John Mathews, Gen. Nathanael Greene, and Gen. William Moultrie. These hardened veterans had survived more than six years of brutal war and knew this would be the end of operations in South Carolina.

Wayne's and Lee's men made it to the outer defenses of Charleston, where the Hessian jaegers made up the British rear guard. Calling out to the Americans to slow their progress because they were just a hundred yards from them, the jaegers slowly fell back to the town. The Americans continued to closely follow. The Hessians fell back through the gates and Hornwork and then marched over to Gadsden's Wharf on the Cooper River where the Royal navy was anchored. Once the last troops made it on board, the British ships, with about 15,000 people (roughly 4,000 British soldiers, 4,000 Loyalists, and 7,000 slaves and free African Americans) sailed off through the harbor and out to sea. Many of them eventually joined the British army in New York City. The Loyalists settled for new lives in various parts of the British Empire

Liberty flags fly in downtown Charleston. (mm)

Liberty Square sits on the location where Gadsden's Wharf once stood and where the British finally evacuated Charleston on December 14, 1782. (mm)

Nathanael Greene, though never having an undisputed victory over the British, was successful in strategically forcing the British out of the South Carolina countryside. He famously said: "We fight, get beat, and fight again." (nypl)

along with the slaves they brought with them, who continued to live in bondage.

Wayne's men marched into the Hornwork and raised the American flag over the defenses of Charleston. Greene's and Moultrie's men marched into the center of town where they were greeted with loud cheers and applause from the inhabitants, who had survived more than two years of British occupation.

Moultrie noted "it was a proud day to me, and I felt myself much elated, at seeing the balconies, the doors, and windows crowded with the patriotic fair [that is, females], the aged citizens and others, congratulating us on our return home, saying 'God bless you, gentlemen! You are welcome home, gentlemen!' Both citizens and soldiers shed mutual tears of joy." Moultrie also proclaimed "This fourteenth day of December, 1782, ought never to be forgotten by the Carolinians; it ought to be a day of festivity with them, as it was the real day of their deliverance and independence."

Greene wrote to the Continental Congress that the city had been liberated and gave all credit to the perseverance of his brave soldiers:

> *"I should be wanting in gratitude to the Army, was I to omit expressing my warmest acknowledgments for the zeal and activity with which they attempted and persevered in every enterprise, and for the*

In 1858, the Washington Light Infantry (a Charleston militia unit), erected this monument to William Washington in one of the city's most prominent burial grounds, Magnolia Cemetery. However, this monument does not mark his actual burial site, which was located on the site of his plantation near Rantowles Bridge. The monument is a beautiful work of art that highlights his service in some of the war's most important battles. (mm)

patience and dignity with which they bore their sufferings. Perhaps no Army ever exhibited greater proofs of patriotism and public virtue. It has been my constant care to alleviate their distresses as much as possible, but my endeavors have been far short of my wishes, or their merit."

When news eventually reached New York, George Washington wished

"to express the sense he entertains of the exalted Merits of the Troops which have been employed in the southern Department, the extraordinary abilities, bravery and prudence displayed by Major General Greene in conducting the operations; the patient virtue and invincible fortitude exhibited by the officers and men in seconding his efforts, amidst innumerable difficulties and hardships, through a long and severe contest, against superior numbers, will entitle them all to the gratitude of their Countrymen, the applause of the present age, and the admiration of posterity."

The city was reinstated as the seat of the South Carolina government. The Patriots took their revenge on many Loyalists by confiscating their land and forcing many into exile. The British army remained in New York City through 1783 until word of the Treaty of Paris arrived in America. New York City was evacuated in November 1783, and in December, George Washington resigned his commission, and the Continental army was ultimately disbanded.

With the war over, South Carolina continued to play an important role in the creation of the American nation, and her Revolutionary War leaders would become major figures; men like John Rutledge, Charles Pinckney, and Charles Cotesworth Pinckney.

Thus closed one of the most important chapters in Charleston's history. The war was over, and Charleston and the United States were finally free and independent. The city of Charleston had witnessed one of the country's earliest victories in June 1776 and had seen its worst defeats in May 1780. To this very day, the palmetto tree and crescent on the South Carolina flag and the annual celebration of Carolina Day are prominent reminders of the city's rich Revolutionary War history. While the victory at Sullivan's Island is still widely celebrated, the efforts of the Patriots between 1779 and 1782 are often overlooked. Those latter years never saw as complete a victory by the Patriots as at Sullivan's Island, but their tenacity and courage should not be ignored. Over the course of more than seven years, the people of Charleston suffered bombardments, death, disease, and hunger through two major battles and dozens of smaller engagements and skirmishes. Men from as far north as Maryland and as far south as Georgia fought in the battles around Charleston. The struggle for this port city resulted in the deaths of thousands of men. Their determination and patience saw the ultimate victory at the war's conclusion. They proved repeatedly that they were willing to defend Charleston and their liberty to the last extremity.

Nearby Associated Sites

While not part of the main tours, these nearby associated sites have connections to the stories around Charleston during the Revolutionary War.

Savannah Battlefield

Though far from Charleston, the battle of Savannah played an important role in the campaign against Charleston and in 1779 was where many prominent Charlestonians fought. In one of the bloodiest assaults in the war, hundreds of American and French troops were mowed down attempting to capture the entrenched British position. Here, heroes like Sgt. William Jasper died carrying the colors of the 2nd South Carolina regiment. Savannah is worth its own trip, and the battlefield park on the site of the Spring Hill Redoubt does a good job interpreting the tragic story of the futile and heroic assault.

303 Martin Luther King, Jr., Blvd.
Savannah, GA 31415
GPS: N 32.075826, W 81.099847

Port Royal Island (Beaufort) Battlefield

This is the site of the battle of Port Royal Island (also known as the battle of Beaufort), which took place on February 3, 1779. The engagement pitted 300 South Carolina militia under William Moultrie against 200 British regulars. The fighting was brief, but fierce. Over the course of 45 minutes, the British lost 40 men killed and wounded and 12 taken prisoner while the South Carolinians lost 7 killed and 18 wounded. Today a historic marker denotes the location where the battle occurred and the graves of two British officers can be found in nearby Beaufort at St. Helena's Church graveyard.

3026 Trask Pkwy, Beaufort, SC 29906
GPS: N 32.477350, W 80.738621

Coosawhatchie Battlefield

Today on the battlefield of Coosawhatchie is a small display describing the brief action that occurred in 1779. (mm)

The battle of Coosawhatchie occurred here on May 3, 1779. Lieutenant Colonel John Laurens took a group of 350 men and attacked Prevost's 2,400-man force. The attack was impetuous and rash. The British poured fire into the small group of Americans, which resulted in a dozen Americans being killed or wounded. Laurens was wounded himself before he ordered his men to fall back to Moultrie's main army two miles northeast at the Tulifiny River. After this action, Moultrie's army retreated towards Charleston, but lost hundreds of men to desertion as they ran to get to their homes to protect them from the approaching British troops. Today at Coosawhatchie, a historic marker interprets the action.

6904 W. Frontage Rd.
Coosawhatchie, SC 29912
GPS: N 32.588379, W 80.926860

Old Sheldon Church Ruins

As Prevost's army marched through the Lowcountry, they burned and pillaged numerous buildings and homes. Among the places burned was the Prince Williams Episcopal Church, today known as the Sheldon Church ruins. After the Revolution, the church was rebuilt, only to be burned in 1865 by Union general William T. Sherman's troops in the American Civil War. Today it stands as a reminder of the cost of war on civilians.

890 Old Sheldon Church Rd.

919 Old Sheldon Church Rd.
Yemassee, SC 29945
GPS: N 32.618528, W 80.780472

John Laurens's Grave

This is the location of the Laurens family plantation, Mepkin Plantation. Today it is operated by Trappist monks as Mepkin Abbey. While the plantation home no longer exists, you can find the Laurens family cemetery here, which includes the graves of Henry Laurens, president of the Continental Congress, and his son John Laurens, who was killed at the battle of Combahee River. John Laurens was an abolitionist South Carolinian who could have played an important role in ending slavery in South Carolina, but because he died far too young we'll never know. His father was imprisoned for a time in the Tower of London during the Revolutionary War, the only American to have been detained there. He survived, returned to Charleston, and interestingly is the first European American to have been purposefully cremated before he was buried in 1792. His infant daughter Martha had nearly been buried alive before it was discovered that she was in fact alive, and Henry Laurens insisted his body be burned for fear of being accidentally buried alive. When his slaves performed the cremation, apparently as his body burned, the head separated from the body and rolled down hill. It was returned and the ashes were buried on the site.

John Laurens is buried next to his father Henry Laurens at their plantation, Mepkin. Engraved on his headstone is the Latin phrase, "Dulce et decorum est pro patria mori," which translates to "It is sweet and fitting to die for one's country." (mw)

1098 Mepkin Abbey Rd.
Moncks Corner, SC 29461
GPS: N 33.117375, W 79.956894

Tomb of Francis Marion

The grave of Francis Marion, "The Swamp Fox." (mm)

Grave of the "Swamp Fox," Francis Marion. Marion was originally an officer in the 2nd South Carolina regiment and took part in the battle of Sullivan's Island in 1776 and the disastrous battle of Savannah in 1779. Avoiding capture at Charleston in 1780, Marion led a group of men in irregular warfare against the British and Loyalists throughout 1780 and 1781. During this time, Marion became known as the "Swamp Fox." The actions of Marion and other partisan fighters helped Nathanael Greene push the British out of the backcountry and ultimately recapture Charleston in 1782. Marion died in 1795.

Snee Farm (Charles Pinckney National Historic Site)

Snee farm was the plantation home of Charles Pinckney, a major figure in the creation of the United States Constitution in 1787. The farm was where William Moultrie was imprisoned following the fall of Charleston in 1780 and where President George Washington had breakfast on the morning of May 2,

1791, during his southern tour. Today, it is a National Park Service site that largely interprets the life and legacy of Charles Pinckney.

1254 Long Point Rd., Mt Pleasant, SC 29464
GPS: N 32.846093, W 79.824654

Eutaw Springs Battlefield

Eutaw Springs was one of the last major battles of the Revolution in South Carolina. As Gen. Nathanael Greene pushed the British closer to Charleston, on September 8, 1781, Greene attacked a British force under the command of Gen. Alexander Stewart. Both forces committed approximately 2,000 men. The fighting was exceptionally vicious and one of the bloodiest of the war with both sides suffering more than 25 percent casualties. Both sides claimed victory, but the British continued to fall back towards to Charleston. While numerous skirmishes would continue over the next year, this marked the last major action. Today, a small park interprets the battle at the site of the heaviest fighting.

12933 Old Number Six Hwy
Eutawville, SC 29048
GPS: N 33.407378, W 80.298517

Today, a small portion of the Eutaw Springs battlefield is preserved as a battlefield park. This was the site of some of the fiercest fighting during the bloody battle and contains some monuments, markers, and the grave of one of the British officers who fought in the battle. (mm)

George Washington Visits Charleston

APPENDIX A

"He comes! he comes! the hero comes.

Sound, sound your trumpets, beat your drums,

From port to port let cannons roar,

His welcome to our friendly shore"

— Song performed for George Washington
as he entered Charleston, May 2, 1791

The first President of the United States, George Washington, made his first and only visit to Charleston in May 1791. Although he spent little more than a week in the city, it was a well-remembered visit that left reminders to this day. The visit was a major event for the city, and all the survivors and heroes from the war came to welcome the American commander in chief. The stop was part of a southern tour of the new United States. Washington, looking to promote unity between the states, also wanted to learn firsthand the South's view of the new Union. The trip lasted for more than three months, covering more than 1,800 miles and going as far south as Savannah, Georgia. The largest city Washington saw on this tour was Charleston, which he visited from May 2 to May 9, 1791.

This portrait of George Washington was commissioned by the city to commemorate George Washington's visit in 1791. A first version of the portrait by John Trumbull was rejected by the city. Trumbull painted a second version that was accepted and hangs today in City Hall. Perhaps as a bit of revenge, Trumbull placed the horse's rear end facing out with its tail raised and the city of Charleston and all the city officials directly underneath the horse's backside. (mm)

After having breakfast at Governor Charles Pinckney's plantation, Snee Farm, Washington proceeded to Haddrell's Point in Mount Pleasant, where he was joined by early political and military leaders such as Revolutionary War general and delegate to the Constitutional Convention Charles Cotesworth Pinckney, Revolutionary War cavalry hero William Washington, and Declaration of Independence signer Edward Rutledge. They then

A view of the Old Exchange Building from the Cooper River. This was the same view Washington had as he came across the river into Charleston in 1791. (mm)

got into a boat with 12 elegantly dressed oarsmen and a captain to make a symbolic 13 seamen (for the 13 original states). As they rowed across the Cooper River towards Charleston, the party was joined by other boats full of well-wishers and people singing songs to the illustrious Washington. Upon their approach to the city, artillery pieces fired salutes and the church bells of St. Michael's rang in honor of the president. Washington landed in Charleston at Prioleau's Wharf (today near Vendue Range). As he entered the city, he saw a massive crowd of thousands that had gathered to greet him. Among the official receiving

The view looking down East Bay Street from Vendue Range. Washington walked down to the Old Exchange Building and reviewed the military units there. (mm)

party were Governor Charles Pinckney, Lt. Governor Isaac Holmes, the Intendant, or mayor of Charleston, both United States senators, the city councilmen, and the local members of the Society of the Cincinnati (former officers of the Continental army). Washington was welcomed by this delegation and escorted down to the Old Exchange Building. From there, Washington watched as the militia marched past him followed by a throng of townspeople. After being thus welcomed to the city, Washington was escorted to his lodgings at

A statue of George Washington, erected in 1999 as part of the bicentennial of George Washington's death, portrays Washington as he looked landing at Prioleau's Wharf on May 2, 1791, and greeting the people of Charleston. (mm)

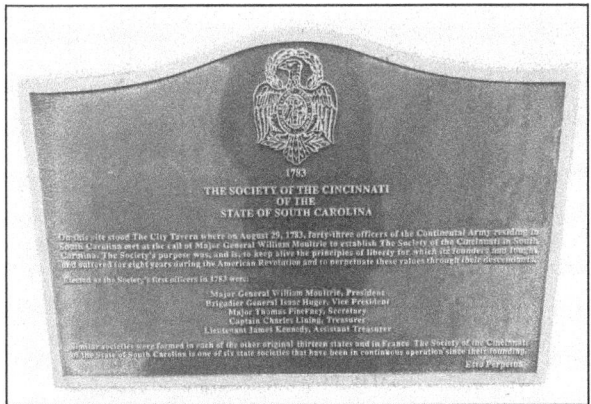

The Society of the Cincinnati (a fraternal organization of Continental army officers formed after the war) organized many of the events during Washington's visit in 1791. This plaque, at the corner of Broad Street and State Street, denotes the location where they originally organized in Charleston. (mm)

The Heyward-Washington House (where Washington stayed while in Charleston) is today a historic house museum operated by the Charleston Museum. (mm)

A plaque on the Heyward-Washington House describes Washington's visit in 1791. (mm)

Thomas Heyward's house, which the city had leased for his use. Washington then dined with Governor Pinckney and several others at Pinckney's home at 16 Meeting Street. The home is no longer there as it was destroyed during the Civil War.

The next morning, May 3, Washington had breakfast at John Rutledge's home. Although Rutledge was not there at the time, Washington was welcomed by Rutledge's wife, Elizabeth. He was then lavishly entertained at the Old Exchange Building in the afternoon by many of the people of Charleston. Toasts were raised, and for every toast to General Washington, an artillery piece would be fired to signal those not personally at the Exchange to toast the General from their homes.

On the morning of May 4, Washington toured the siege lines where Lincoln's army had put up a vigorous defense in 1780. He noted in his diary that "I visited and examined the lines of Attack & defence of the City and was satisfied that the defence was noble & honorable altho the measure was undertaken upon wrong principles and impolitic." That afternoon, Washington dined at McCrady's tavern with the local Society of the Cincinnati. In the evening, he attended a ball at the Old Exchange Building, where he noted that there "were 256 elegantly dressed & handsome ladies." Many of the women wore ribbons and sashes that read "Long Live the President" or "GW."

On May 5, Washington, escorted by Gen. William Moultrie, toured the harbor by visiting Fort Johnson and Fort Moultrie, which he noted were both "in ruins, and scarcely a trace of the latter left." That evening he dined at Governor Pinckney's and then attended a concert at the Old Exchange Building where he noted in his diary that it was attended by "at

George Washington had breakfast at the John Rutledge House. (mm)

The Long Room where Washington ate dinner on May 4, 1791. (mm)

Washington was entertained multiple times at the Old Exchange Building during his visit to Charleston in 1791. (mm)

least 400 ladies—the Number & appearances of wch. exceeded any thing of the kind I had ever seen."

On May 6, Washington rode through the city on horseback, and that evening dined with Senator Pierce Butler before attending a ball at Governor Pinckney's home on Meeting Street.

The following day, May 7, Washington visited the Orphan House, which was temporarily near present-day Market Street and Meeting Street. He then visited St. Michael's Church and ascended into the church steeple to view the city and countryside from that vantage point. He enjoyed the view and noted the beauty of the city. That evening he again had a feast at the Old Exchange Building, and following the dinner enjoyed fireworks over the harbor.

The Calhoun Mansion sits on the site of Governor Pinckney's mansion where Washington was entertained in 1791. (mm)

On Sunday, May 8, Washington attended church at St. Phillip's in the morning and St. Michael's in the afternoon. That evening he had a private dinner with William Moultrie.

McCrady's Tavern was where Washington was entertained on May 4, 1791. (mm)

Washington prepared to leave Charleston on May 9. He rode with most of the leading citizens of Charleston out of the city and exchanged pleasantries and goodbyes near Boundary Street (Calhoun Street). He then rode to a bridge near Bees Ferry. At the bridge over the Ashley River was a large wooden triumphal arch that was constructed for him. Washington crossed the Ashley and headed to Sandy Hill plantation, where he stayed the night with his distant cousin, William Washington. The next day, Washington continued his southern tour toward Savannah.

Washington was pleased with his visit to Charleston and described the people of the city as "wealthy—Gay—& hospitable; appear happy, & satisfied with the Genl. Governmt." He believed the people gave him "very polite attention" and he noted that "it will give me pleasure to visit again this very respectable city."

As for the people of Charleston, they long remembered and venerated the visit Washington paid them. Today, visitors can see the home he stayed in during his visit, tour the Old Exchange Building

The famous Charleston City Market was not constructed until the 1840s. Today, the Daughters of the Confederacy operate a Civil War museum in the old market hall.
The Orphan House that Washington visited in 1791, at one time was in a building located near the North Market Street and Church Street where a parking lot is today. (mm)

where so much of his time was spent, and see one of the churches where he worshipped while in town. Additionally, a statue depicting Washington entering the city now stands in Washington Square Park behind City Hall. Inside of City Hall hangs a portrait of Washington at Charleston, painted by John Trumbull. The painting was commissioned by the city during Washington's visit.

The visit to Charleston allowed Washington to see this part of the country that he had never seen before. In the end, Washington had succeeded in helping to promote national unity and, in the very early days of the federal republic, a belief in the new American government.

Revolutionary War Charleston in American Memory

APPENDIX B

Charleston is a city that loves its history. It has remembered with pride some of the major events and personalities of the Revolutionary War. South Carolina heroes Francis Marion, Thomas Sumter, John Laurens, William Moultrie, and William Jasper became household names. However, not all the city's history has been well remembered. Beginning during the war, the amazing events of June 28, 1776 at Sullivan's Island were celebrated by Charlestonians, while the rest of the war's events went largely forgotten.

Before the first anniversary of the battle of Sullivan's Island, the people of Charleston formed the Palmetto Society in 1777. This group was created to celebrate "the signal and providential victory obtained by our gallant troops, over the formidable fleet and army of Great Britain, at Sullivan's Island." The celebrations continued annually every June 28 throughout the "arduous struggle for liberty" until the city was captured by the British in 1780. Following the liberation of the city in 1782, the celebrations started up again.

These celebrations often vied in size with July 4 in Charleston throughout the eighteenth and early nineteenth centuries. While the victory of June 28 was proudly celebrated and remembered, the near defeat in 1779 and total defeat in 1780 went largely ignored. The actions of 1779 and the humiliating defeat in 1780 were embarrassing, even though the Continentals had put up a noble fight in both instances. Even the jubilant liberation of the city by Gen. Nathanael Greene and his army in 1782 was largely forgotten. Why was this? Why was the victory of 1776 celebrated and the actions of the later part of the war forgotten?

A big part of the reason likely was the fact that the 1776 battle was a victory. It is easier to celebrate victories than defeats. Another important reason was

This drawing from *Harper's Weekly* depicts the Defenders of Fort Moultrie monument in White Point Garden that was dedicated on the centennial of the battle in 1876. The figure of Jasper holds the flag and points to Fort Moultrie across the harbor. (hw)

likely the composition and leadership of the 1776 battle versus the later events. The victory in 1776 was accomplished largely by South Carolina forces, under the command of a South Carolina officer, Col. William Moultrie. Especially as the sectional crisis grew in the nineteenth century, South Carolinians clung with pride to their history of helping to secure America's independence. South Carolina could proudly point to the victory at Sullivan's Island as uniquely their own. The later battles of the Revolution around Charleston had much more diverse armies with men from Delaware all the way to Georgia engaged and they were led by Northerners: Gen. Benjamin Lincoln of Massachusetts and Gen. Nathanael Greene of Rhode Island. The the people of the South were very grateful for the service of Nathanael Greene that they gave him a plantation in Georgia near Savannah after the war. Unfortunately, not long after he moved permanently to Georgia, he died of sunstroke in 1786 and is today buried in a downtown square in Savannah, Georgia. While Greene's Fabian strategy of keeping his army together proved ultimately successful, he never had a complete battlefield victory quite as dramatic as the victory at Sullivan's Island.

Even though the victory at Sullivan's Island was remembered, the actual battlefields around Charleston went largely neglected following the war. Even as early as George Washington's visit in 1791 the palmetto fort on Sullivan's Island had rotted away and the extensive 1780 siege lines near downtown Charleston were filled in.

While the sites perished, the heroic deeds, specifically of the Patriots at Sullivan's Island, continued to be celebrated up until the American Civil War. Often there were parades and speeches in downtown Charleston, but also out at the site of the battle at Fort Moultrie, which was rebuilt by the United States Army and continued to be used by the military into the twentieth century. Many of the public addresses and orations on the battle anniversary said more about the contemporaneous political issues than about the actual battle itself. The fact that the battle was fought solely by South Carolina troops served not only as a source of regional pride but also reinforced a popular belief that South Carolina could stand on her own. As South Carolina plunged into the Nullification Crisis of the 1830s and then into the secession crisis of the 1850s, the holiday served

as a connection between the present and the past. In fact, some of the speeches at the event became so celebratory of the idea of secession in 1850 that in 1851, the federal garrison stationed at Fort Moultrie, refused to let locals celebrate the battle anniversary at the fort. The following years they were able to hold the ceremonies again, but the speeches became more tempered as the nation hurtled towards Civil War.

A Confederate soldier at Fort Moultrie dreams of the heroes of Sullivan's Island while stationed at Fort Moultrie. (hw)

On December 20, 1860, South Carolina officially seceded from the Union. The South Carolina Secession Convention held its vote in downtown Charleston. The only federal soldiers in the area were less than 100 soldiers under the command of Maj. Robert Anderson stationed at Fort Moultrie. Fort Moultrie once again became front page news in 1860 when it became the epicenter of the standoff in Charleston Harbor. On December 26, 1860, Anderson moved his garrison from Fort Moultrie to Fort Sumter in the middle of the harbor. South Carolina troops took over Fort Moultrie. The standoff lasted until April 12, 1861, when a signal shot was fired by South Carolina troops from Fort Johnson to let all southern batteries in the harbor know to commence firing. Thus, some of the first shots of the American Civil War were fired at Fort Sumter from the venerable Fort Moultrie.

Both sides saw the symbolism of the Revolutionary War history that occurred in the same harbor less than a hundred years earlier. At one point in the 1861 battle, the American flag in Fort Sumter was shot away, and Sgt. Peter Hart from New York took the flag and nailed it back on the mast under a hail of fire, not unlike Sgt. William Jasper in 1776. In the *West Jersey Pioneer Newspaper* in May 1861, the paper noted, "the same spirit that actuated Jasper of revolutionary renown, at Fort Moultrie, to nail fast the colors that had been shot down by the foe, inspired the brave Hart of New York when, a few rods only from the scene of Jasper's adventures, when he replaced the stars and stripes, amid the whizzing balls of the enemy."

On the Confederate side, a similar event occurred in 1863 when Union ships launched an attack on Fort Sumter and Fort Moultrie. At one point a Union cannonball knocked the First National Confederate flag to the ground, the flagpole killing a man when it went down. Immediately, a Confederate soldier pulled the flag off the fallen mast, and near the same spot Jasper performed his heroic feat, stood on the wall of the fort holding the flag afloat until a new pole was put up. He "stood under the heavy fire immovable" and survived the action.

Formal celebrations of the Revolutionary War battle largely disappeared during the American Civil War and in the years immediately following it. In 1866, the *Charleston Daily News* noted sorrowfully that while the day had previously been largely celebrated as a great holiday for freedom, "self-government, for us, is gone." But the newspaper remembered fondly "the social reunions by which it has been so often marked." They hoped that the men "who more recently stood shoulder to shoulder in the hardships and danger of real war, would unite to perpetuate the bonds of friendship so solemnly cemented." Beginning in the 1870s, South Carolinians and Charlestonians began to mark the events of Sullivan's Island annually again. These remembrances culminated in a large celebration

SERGEANT HART NAILING THE COLORS TO THE FLAGSTAFF OF FORT SUMTER.

In a heroic feat similar to that of Sgt. William Jasper, Peter Hart repaired the American flag in Fort Sumter that was shot down by Confederate forces. (hw)

at Fort Moultrie on the 100th anniversary in 1876. Men from Massachusetts and New York joined the men from South Carolina in celebrating the history of this event. The keynote address was delivered by former Confederate general Joseph B. Kershaw, who commanded the 2nd South Carolina Regiment in the Confederate army and saw major action throughout the Civil War. The spirit of the event was very much in favor of reconciliation between North and South at Fort Moultrie. After having spent four years in fratricidal war, Northerners and Southerners looked to bury old animosities and join in rebuilding the United States as it entered its one hundredth year. In looking at the victory of 1776, they saw it now as not only as part of South Carolina's history, but a symbol of how South Carolina helped to establish the recently re-United States. The shared Revolutionary War history of the nation became a unifying symbol.

Former Confederate general Joseph B. Kershaw was the keynote speaker at the centennial celebration of the battle of Sullivan's Island in 1876. (wiki)

The same year, in 1876, a new monument was unveiled in downtown Charleston on the Battery to the 2nd South Carolina Regiment at the battle of Sullivan's Island. Atop the monument was erected a statue of Sgt. William Jasper holding the flag he so proudly saved in 1776.

The people of South Carolina continued celebrating June 28 throughout the twentieth century and now into the twenty-first century. Originally called Palmetto Day, it is mostly referred to today as Carolina Day. In 2007, a statue of William Moultrie was placed on the Battery nearby the monument to the 2nd South Carolina. The figure of Moultrie stares from the Battery off towards Sullivan's Island and the site of his greatest victory. Every year on the anniversary of the battle, to this day, celebrations are held in downtown Charleston and on Sullivan's Island.

While it is good that the victory of June 28, 1776, is remembered and celebrated, it is hoped that this book will help Americans remember the people and places associated not just with the June 28 battle, but the important engagements in 1779, 1780, and the sacrifice of patriots from 1780 in and around the city of Charleston. While it is not as easy to celebrate the defeat and privation suffered, it should be remembered and honored since victory is not the only measure by which to judge history.

In 1849, a South Carolina newspaper, *The Edgefield Advertiser*, summed up the importance of remembering the Revolutionary War history of Charleston and

This newspaper drawing depicts a scene that occurred at Fort Moultrie in 1863 as a Confederate soldier bravely holds a first national Confederate flag aloft during a bombardment by Union gunboats. (cc)

South Carolina, whether in victory or defeat. They said that the celebrations of the battle of Sullivan's Island are good as they "have a happy effect on the young and warm the hearts of the old. They store the mind with patriotic sentiments and inspire it with noble and heroic impulses." And, "every spot in the country where our fathers bled should be consecrated to their memories – to patriotism and valor." Though many of Charleston's battlefields were the scenes of tragic defeats, the courage and sacrifice of the soldiers deserves recognition and honor.

THE BATTLES FOR CHARLESTON

THE BATTLE FOR SULLIVAN'S ISLAND
June 28, 1776

SOUTHERN CONTINENTAL ARMY
Gen. Charles Lee

Fort on Sullivan's Island: Col. William Moultrie
2nd South Carolina • 4th South Carolina detachment of Artillery

Breach Inlet: Lt. Col. William "Danger" Thomson
3rd South Carolina Rifles • 1st North Carolina • South Carolina Militia
"Raccoon" Company • Charleston Militia • Artillery

Haddrell's Point: Brig. Gen. James Armstrong
5th South Carolina • 6th South Carolina • 1st North Carolina
2nd North Carolina • 8th Virginia • Charleston Artillery

Fort Johnson: Col. Christopher Gadsden
1st South Carolina

Charleston
South Carolina Militia • Charleston Militia • 3rd North Carolina
4th South Carolina

ROYAL NAVY
Comm. Peter Parker

Bristol (50-gun frigate) • *Experiment* (50-gun frigate) • *Active* (28-gun frigate)
Solebay (28-gun frigate) • *Acteon* (28-gun frigate) • *Syren* (28-gun frigate)
Sphinx (20-gun frigate) • *Friendship* (22-gun armed transport) • *Thunder* (8-gun
bombship) • *Ranger* (8-gun sloop) • *St. Lawrence* (8-gun schooner)

BRITISH ARMY
Gen. Henry Clinton

15th Regiment of Foot • 33rd Regiment of Foot • 37th Regiment of Foot
42nd Regiment of Foot • 54th Regiment of Foot • 57th Regiment of Foot
Royal Marines

PREVOST'S INVASION
MAY 11–12, 1779

SOUTHERN CONTINENTAL ARMY
Brig. Gen. William Moultrie

1st South Carolina • 2nd South Carolina • 4th South Carolina
5th South Carolina • Colonel Harris Light Infantry • Pulaski's American Legion

Militia
Charleston Militia • French Company • Country Militia • Charleston Artillery
Beaufort Militia • Colonel Neal's Regiment • "Raccoon" Company

BRITISH ARMY
Gen. Augustine Prevost

1st Battalion, 71st Regiment of Foot • Regiment von Wissenbach
2nd Battalion DeLancy's • North and South Carolina Provincials
Grenadier Corps of the Florida Brigade • Regiment von Wollwarth
Light Dragoons • Light Infantry Corps • New York Volunteers • Creek Indians

THE SIEGE OF CHARLESTON
FEBRUARY–MAY 1780

SOUTHERN CONTINENTAL ARMY
Gen. Benjamin Lincoln

Moultrie's Brigade: Brig. Gen. William Moultrie
1st South Carolina • 2nd South Carolina • 3rd South Carolina

Hogun's Brigade: Brig. Gen. James Hogun
1st North Carolina • 2nd North Carolina • 3rd North Carolina • Light Infantry

Parker's Brigade: Col. Richard Parker
1st Virginia (detachment) • 2nd Virginia (detachment) • North Carolina Militia

Light Dragoons

Woodford's Brigade: Brig. Gen. William Woodford
1st Virginia • 2nd Virginia • 3rd Virginia

Charleston Brigade: Col. Maurice Simons
Charleston Militia • French Company

McIntosh's Brigade: Brig. Gen. Lachlan McIntosh
North Carolina Militia • South Carolina Militia

Lillington's Brigade: Brig. Gen. Alexander Lillington
South Carolina Militia

Harrington's Brigade: Brig. Gen. William Harrington
North Carolina Militia

Read's Brigade: Col. James Read
North Carolina Militia • Virginia Militia

Brigade of Artillery: Col. Barnard Beekman
4th South Carolina • North Carolina Regiment of Artillery • Charleston Battalion of Artillery • Company of Cannoneers • Virginia State Artillery Regiment

Fort Moultrie: Col. Charles Cotesworth Pinckney
1st South Carolina

CONTINENTAL NAVY
Comm. Abraham Whipple

Continental Navy ships
Ranger (20-gun sloop) • *Queen of France* (28-gun frigate) • *Providence* (32-gun sloop) *Boston* (46-gun frigate)

South Carolina state ships
Bricole (44-gun frigate) • *General Moultrie* (20-gun schooner) • *Notre Dame* (16-gun brig) • *Marquis de Britigney* (7-gun galley) • *Lee* (12-gun galley) *Revenge* (7-gun galley)

French Navy ships
L'Aventure (26-gun sloop) • *Truite* (26-gun sloop) • *Zephyr* (18-gun polacre)

BRITISH ARMY
Gen. Henry Clinton

Light Infantry and Grenadiers: Maj. Gen. Alexander Leslie
Light Infantry Corps: 1st Battalion • 2nd Battalion
Grenadier Corps: 1st Battalion • 2nd Battalion
Royal Regiment of Artillery

Clarke's Brigade: Lt. Col. Alured Clarke
7th Regiment of Foot • 23rd Regiment of Foot

Webster's Corps: Lt. Col. James Webster
33rd Regiment of Foot • Hesse-Kassel Field Jaeger Corps
Field Jaeger Regiment Anspach-Beyreuth

Huyne's Brigade: Maj. Gen. Christoph von Huyne
63rd Regiment of Foot • 64th Regiment of Foot • Hesse-Kassel Garrison
Regiment von Benning • 60th (Royal American) Regiment of Foot

German Forces
Jaegers • Grenadier Regiment von Linsing • Grenadier Regiment von Lengereke
Grenadier Regiment von Minnigerode • Grenadier Regiment von Graff
Grenadier Regiment von Huyne • German Artillery

Patterson's Brigade: Brig. Gen. James Patterson
71st Regiment of Foot • Major Graham's Light Infantry Corps
17th Light Dragoons

Provincial Forces
British Legion • Ferguson's American Volunteers • South Carolina Royalists
North Carolina Volunteers • New York Volunteers • King's American Regiment

Westerhagen's Brigade: Col. Max von Westerhagen
42nd Regiment of Foot • Hessian Regiment von Dittfurth • Queen's Rangers
Prince of Wales' Loyal American Volunteers • Volunteers of Ireland

ROYAL NAVY
Adm. Mariot Arbuthnot

Russell (74-gun ship of the line) • *Robust* (74-gun ship of the line)
Europe (64-gun ship of the line) • *Raisonable* (64-gun ship of the line)
Renown (50-gun ship of the line) • *Romulus* (44-gun ship of the line)
Roebuck (44-gun frigate) • *Blonde* (32-gun frigate) • *Redmond* (32-gun frigate)
Raleigh (28-gun frigate) • *Virginia* (28-gun frigate) • *Perseus* (20-gun frigate)
Camilla (20-gun frigate) • *Vigilant* (18-gun schooner) • Provincial ship
Germaine (20-gun sloop) • Armed galleys • Transport ships

Suggested Reading

THE BATTLES FOR CHARLESTON

A Gallant Defense: The Siege of Charleston, 1780
Carl P. Borick
University of South Carolina, 2003
ISBN: 1570034877

Borick's book is the definitive work on the 1780 siege of Charleston. Well-researched and well-written, it is an in-depth look at Charleston from February to May of 1780.

Relieve Us of this Burthen: American Prisoners of War in the Revolutionary South, 1780–1782
Carl P. Borick
University of South Carolina, 2012
ISBN: 1611170397

A book focused on the plight of prisoners of war in Charleston during the Revolutionary War. Often overlooked, the prisoners severely suffered during the conflict.

Crescent Moon over *Carolina: William Moultrie &
American Liberty*
C. L. Bragg
University of South Carolina, 2013
ISBN: 16111726915

Bragg's book is a good biography of William
Moultrie, who played a central role in the
Revolutionary War in South Carolina, and
especially around Charleston.

*The Road to Guilford Courthouse: The American
Revolution in the Carolinas*
John Buchanan
University of Michigan, 1997
ISBN: 0471327166

Buchanan's work is a great introduction to the
Southern campaign of the Revolutionary War.
Easy to read, Buchanan follows the campaign
from the battle of Sullivan's Island in 1776 up
to the battle of Guilford Courthouse in 1781.
It contextualizes the actions around Charleston
within the partisan fighting that broke out in the
backcountry between the fall of Charleston and
the battle at Guilford.

The Road to Charleston
John Buchanan
University of Virginia, 2019
ISBN: 0813947545

A continuation of his early work, the narrative
begins in the immediate aftermath of Guilford
Courthouse and continues to the liberation of
Charleston in December of 1782.

South Carolina and the American Revolution:
A Battlefield History
John W. Gordon
University of South Carolina, 2003
ISBN: 1570036616

A good military history of the major actions
throughout the war in South Carolina. It is a good
introduction to South Carolina's Revolutionary
War history.

The Revolutionary War Walking History
Mary Clark Coy
Self-Published, 2009
ISBN: N/A

Coy's book is great for people who enjoy strolling
the historic streets of Charleston. This is the only
guidebook of downtown Charleston that focuses
exclusively on the city's rich Revolutionary War
history.

South Carolina in 1791: George Washington's
Southern Tour
Terry W. Lipscomb
South Carolina Department of
Archives and History, 1993
ISBN: 1880067226

Lipscomb's book is a great history on President
Washington's 1791 tour through South Carolina.
There is in-depth information on his visit
specifically to Charleston with plenty of images
and maps.

Fort Moultrie: Official National Park Handbook
Jim Stokeley
National Park Service, 1985
ISBN: 0912627271

This is the National Park Service's handbook for
Fort Moultrie. The heavily-illustrated book covers
the entire history of the site from the colonial days
past World War II. It includes a good retelling of
the June 28, 1776, battle.

The Southern Strategy
David K. Wilson
University of South Carolina, 2005
ISBN: 1570035733

Wilson's book is a great study on the battles and
campaigns in the South from 1775 to 1780. The
work examines ten battles including Sullivan's
Island, Prevost's invasion, and the siege of
Charleston and includes well-researched battle
maps and orders of battle.

*Nothing But Blood and Slaughter: The Revolutionary War
in the Carolinas, 1771–1782*
Patrick O'Kelley
Booklocker.com, Inc., 2004
ISBN: 1591134587

Patrick O'Kelley's books are amazing reference
resources. He has compiled massive amounts of
information on nearly every known battle and
skirmish that occurred in the Carolinas during
the Revolutionary War and provides contextual
information about them as well.

All That Can Be Expected

The Battle of Camden and the British High Tide in the South, August 16, 1870

By the spring of 1780 war raged in the American south. In Georgia, the city of Savannah and most of the colony was already under Royal control. In mid-May, after a months-long siege, British forces under the command of Lt. Gen. Sir Henry Clinton successfully captured the city of Charlestown, South Carolina, thus handing the Continental army its worst defeat of the war.

By summer, with hopes of turning the tables and bolstering the Patriot war effort, American Continental troops from Maryland and Delaware, commanded by the German-born Maj. Gen. Baron de Kalb, marched south. Joining with militia forces from North Carolina and Virginia, this Patriot army was now under the overall leadership of the newly appointed commander of the Southern Department, Maj. Gen. Horatio Gates.

Coming Fall 2023

Siding with the Patriot forces, Horatio Gates brought years of military experience to the Continental army. In the fall of 1777, he gained a stunning victory over a British army under Maj. Gen. John Burgoyne at the battle of Saratoga. Now commanding the Patriot forces in the South, in mid-august 1780 Horatio Gates marched his "Grand Army" toward the strategic British military outpost of Camden, South Carolina. Unbeknownst to the "Hero of Saratoga," his mixed force of experienced Continental veterans and green, untested militia was on a collision course with some of the most experienced and well-trained troops in the British army. In command of these troops was the brilliant Lt. Gen. Charles, Earl Cornwallis.

Though a major defeat for the Patriot forces, the battle of Camden ultimately proved to be the high tide of success for British efforts in the South.

In _All That Can Be Expected_, authors Robert Orrison and Mark Wilcox recount not only the events leading up to the August 16, 1780, battle of Camden, but also the rise of the Patriot partisan leaders Francis Marion, Thomas Sumter, and others who continued the fight in the South Carolina backcountry, thus hampering the efforts of Lord Cornwallis to pacify the southern states.

Unhappy Catastrophes

The Battles of Lexington and Concord and the Beginning of the American Revolution, April 19, 1775

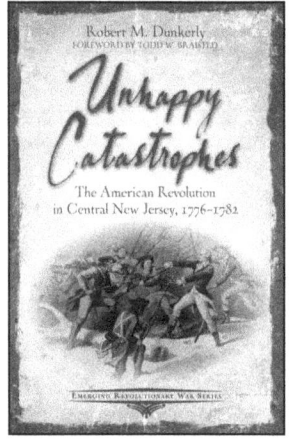

"The Importance of the North River (the Hudson), and the sanguine wishes of all to prevent the enemy from possessing it, have been the causes of this unhappy catastrophe." So wrote General George Washington in 1776 as the British invaded New Jersey. Worse was to come, as the British overran the state, and the Americans suffered one unhappy catastrophe after another.

Central New Jersey witnessed many small battles and important events during the American Revolution. This area saw it all: from spies and espionage, to military encampments like Morristown and Middlebrook, to mutinies, raids, and full-blown engagements like Bound Brook, Short Hills, and Springfield. The British had their own catastrophes too. So did civilians caught in the middle.

In the fall of 1776, British forces drove the Americans out and secured the state. Following the battles of Trenton and Princeton, New Jersey became a battleground. The spring of 1777 saw the formation of a new Continental Army, one that served the rest of the war. That spring, British and American forces clashed in a series of small but sharp battles. By summer, British General Howe tried to lure Washington into a major engagement, but the Americans avoided the trap. As the conflict dragged on, civilians became engulfed in the fray, and a bitter civil war erupted, continuing until the end of the conflict.

In *Unhappy Catastrophes: The American Revolution in Central New Jersey, 1776–1782*, Robert M. Dunkerly follows the course of the war through its various phases and details lesser-known battles, military campsites, raids, espionage, and more. The book also includes historic sites to visit, markers, and websites for further research and study. This part of New Jersey saw more action during the Revolution than anywhere else in the young nation and has been called the Cockpit of the Revolution. To truly understand the war, look at central New Jersey.

The Winter that Won the War

The Winter Encampment at Valley Forge, 1777–1778

"An Army of skeletons appeared before our eyes naked, starved, sick and discouraged."

Gouverneur Morris recorded these words in his report to the Continental Congress after a visit to the Continental Army encampment at Valley Forge. Sent as part of a fact-finding mission, Morris and his fellow congressmen arrived to conditions far worse than they had initially expected.

After a campaigning season that saw the defeat at Brandywine, the loss of Philadelphia, the capital of the rebellious British North American colonies, and the reversal at Germantown, George Washington and his harried army marched into Valley Forge on December 19, 1777.

What transpired in the next six months prior to the departure from the winter cantonment on June 19, 1778 was truly remarkable. The stoic Virginian, George Washington solidified his hold on the army and endured political intrigue, the quartermaster department was revived with new leadership from a former Rhode Island Quaker, and a German baron trained the army in the rudiments of being a soldier and military maneuvers.

Valley Forge conjures up images of cold, desperation, and starvation. Yet Valley Forge also became the winter of transformation and improvement that set the Continental Army on the path to military victory and the fledgling nation on the path to independence.

In The Winter that Won the War: The Winter Encampment at Valley Forge, 1777-1778, historian Phillip S. Greenwalt takes the reader on campaign in the year 1777 and through the winter encampment, detailing the various changes that took place within Valley Forge that ultimately led to the success of the American cause. Walk with the author through 1777 and into 1778 and see how these months truly were the winter that won the war.

A Handsome Flogging

The Battle of Monmouth, June 28, 1778

June 1778 was a tumultuous month in the annals of American military history. Somehow, General George Washington and the Continental Army were able to survive a string of defeats around Philadelphia in 1777 and a desperate winter at Valley Forge. As winter turned to spring, and spring turned to summer, the army—newly trained by Baron von Steuben and in high spirits thanks to France's intervention into the conflict—marched out of Valley Forge in pursuit of Henry Clinton's British Army making its way across New Jersey for New York City.

What would happen next was not an easy decision for Washington to make. Should he attack the British column? And if so, how? "People expect something from us and our strength demands it," Gen. Nathanael Greene pressed his chieftain. Against the advice of many of his subordinates, Washington ordered the army to aggressively pursue the British and not allow the enemy to escape to New York City without a fight.

On June 28, 1778, the vanguard of the Continental Army under Maj. Gen. Charles Lee engaged Clinton's rearguard near the small village of Monmouth Court House. Lee's over-cautiousness prevailed and the Americans were ordered to hasty retreat. Only the arrival of Washington and the main body of the army saved the Americans from disaster. By the end of the day, they held the field as the British continued their march to Sandy Hook and New York City.

In *A Handsome Flogging: The Battle of Monmouth, June 28, 1778*, historian William Griffith retells the story of what many historians have dubbed the "battle that made the American army," and takes you along the routes trekked by both armies on their marches toward destiny. Follow in the footsteps of heroes (and a heroine) who, on a hot summer day, met in desperate struggle in the woods and farm fields around Monmouth Court House.

Victory or Death

The Battles of Trenton and Princeton, December 25, 1776—January 3, 1777

December 1776: Just six months after the signing of the Declaration of Independence, George Washington and the new American Army sit on the verge of utter destruction by the banks of the Delaware River. The despondent and demoralized group of men had endured repeated defeats and now were on the edge of giving up hope. Washington feared "the game is pretty near up."

Rather than submit to defeat, Washington and his small band of soldiers crossed the ice-choked Delaware River and attacked the Hessian garrison at Trenton, New Jersey, on the day after Christmas. He followed up the surprise attack with successful actions along the Assunpink Creek and at Princeton. In a stunning military campaign, Washington had turned the tables, and breathed life into the dying cause for liberty during the Revolutionary War.

The campaign has led many historians to deem it as one of the most significant military campaigns in American history. One British historian even declared that "it may be doubted whether so small a number of men ever employed so short a space of time with greater or more lasting results upon the history of the world."

In *Victory or Death*, historian Mark Maloy not only recounts these epic events, he takes you along to the places where they occurred. He shows where Washington stood on the banks of the Delaware and contemplated defeat, the city streets that his exhausted men charged through, and the open fields where Washington himself rode into the thick of battle. Victory or Death is a must for anyone interested in learning how George Washington and his brave soldiers grasped victory from the jaws of defeat.

About the Author

Mark Maloy is a historian and currently works for the National Park Service in Virginia. He holds an undergraduate degree in History from the College of William and Mary and a graduate degree in History from George Mason University. He has worked at numerous public historic sites and archaeological digs for the past fifteen years. He is a Revolutionary War reenactor and resides in Stafford, Virginia, with his wife, Lauren, and sons, Samuel and Thomas.